KPF

Selected and Current Works

KPF

Selected and Current Works

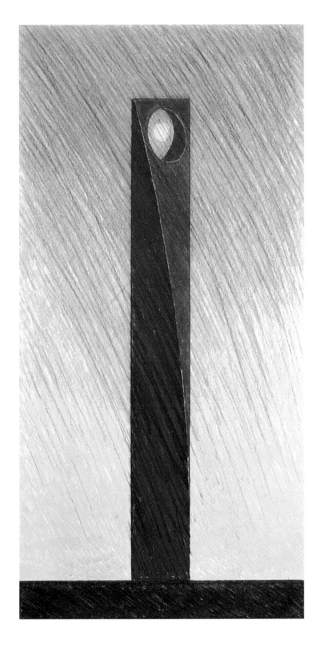

First published in Australia in 1997 by
The Images Publishing Group Pty Ltd
ACN 059 734 431
6 Bastow Place, Mulgrave, Victoria, 3170
Telephone (61 3) 9561 5544 Facsimile (61 3) 9561 4860

National Library of Australia Cataloguing-in-Publication Data

KPF: selected and current works.

Bibliography.
Includes index.
ISBN 1 875498 58 3.

1. Kohn Pedersen Fox Associates PC. (Firm). 2. Architecture, American.
3. Architecture, Modern—20th century—United
States. 4. Architects, American. I. Title: Kohn Pedersen Fox.
(Series: Master architect series 2).

720.92

Edited by Stephen Dobney
Designed by The Graphic Image Studio Pty Ltd,
Mulgrave, Australia
Film by Scanagraphix Australia Pty Ltd
Printing by Everbest Printing, Hong Kong

Contents

Contents Continued

INTRODUCTION

Preface

The Partners of Kohn Pedersen Fox have always provided the inspiration, leadership, and opportunity in our pursuit of one dominant objective: to produce architecture of the highest quality. It is our belief that the quality of the whole is equal to the quality of the sum of its parts in both our work and organizational structure. Our process and our practice have evolved to meet this objective.

This book is a celebration of the work of KPF and, most importantly, an acknowledgment of the process by which we create distinctive architecture. The format is a departure from that of previous publications of our work and as such is intended to reveal a closer view of both the structure of our firm and the process that has led to a significant body of work.

Introduction
By Gregory Clement
AIA, Principal

There is neither a formal credo nor a rigid organizational structure by which we practice architecture at KPF. There is not a single guiding hand overseeing the creation and execution of the work. We work within a conceptual framework with few boundaries limiting the exploration of any particular design challenge. Our structure has deliberately evolved throughout the firm's 21-year history to best exploit our diverse and changing talents. There are philosophical and organizational threads that bind the fabric of the office and its intentions. They are most apparent in the measure of responsibility that is entrusted in the senior architects, as evidenced by their work, and in the potential for participation and creative expression available to every member of a project team.

To be able to meet the complex and varied demands of designing and building both large and small scale projects, we have created an environment that possesses the intimacy of a small studio combined with the resources of a large, highly proficient office. By assigning the responsibility for all aspects of a project to a single dedicated team for the duration of a project, we engender in each member of that team the ambition to participate in a meaningful way in the development of the work. This is the collaborative spirit from which our best work emerges, and it sponsors a palpable sense of pride in each individual's contribution and in the collective efforts of the project team, who perhaps will work together as a group only once. This is vital to our success. We strongly believe that it is due to each members personal investment in their contribution to the work that the work is made better. It is evident in the smallest detail of a project, such as in the refinement of a door pull, that acknowledges the larger intentions of the design yet clearly has the unique imprint of its designer.

The success of any project also involves the influences of forces beyond the talents in our office. They include the clients who seek innovative solutions, historical sources that are the intuitive underpinnings of our search, and of course elements of climate, orientation, and context. The thorough analysis and balancing of all of these influences is the essence of our design process, and leads to the uniqueness of each solution. We work in a comparative method, preparing alternative studies, always striving to engage these often disparate forces into a three-dimensional equilibrium that, in the final solution, exceeds the project goals.

We consider the client to be an essential collaborator in the development of a project. It is only through understanding the clients' needs and aspirations and encouraging their participation in the design process that a truly great work of architecture can emerge. We seek this involvement from a project's inception and encourage continuing participation, throughout the ensuing phases.

KPF is clearly a global practice, as evidenced by the scope of work completed and currently under design. Essential to the success of these projects is that they are not designed in satellite offices scattered throughout the world, but only in offices in New York and London. By concentrating the focus of our creative efforts in just two locations, all of the fundamental aspects of our practice remain intact and the work is more clearly identifiable as part of the same family. While this puts a tremendous pressure on the firm's resources, we believe it is the only way to ensure consistency in the quality of our work.

We have evolved to be able to adapt to the varied challenges presented by the diverse cultures in which we work. These include not only the professional cultures endemic to corporations, developers, academic institutions, governments, or the arts, but also the cultures of the people of different states and nations that are manifested in the history, customs, religion, language, and societies of each place.

The evidence of programmatic and/or cultural influences playing a role in our creative response is most apparent in projects such as the Bank Niaga Headquarters in Jakarta, Indonesia, which includes a mosque as an integral part of the program and consequent composition of a corporate headquarters. The design of the First Hawaiian Bank in Honolulu cleverly addresses local zoning regulations by locating the elevators at the exterior of the building, thereby maximizing the internal floor area potential and, in addition, integrates a branch of the Honolulu Museum of Contemporary Art as part of its main banking hall, as if the two were always meant to be together. The form and material of the IBM Headquarters in Armonk, New York, reflect not only the past growth of a preeminent technology corporation but an expression of its future as the leader in that industry. The Rodin Pavilion in Seoul, Korea, creates a transcendent environment for two masterpieces of 20th century sculpture by August Rodin contained within a structure made entirely of glass. Lastly, the Foley Square and Portland courthouses not only meet the demanding requirements of Federal courts buildings, they are expressions of civic pride in our judicial system and in the cities in which they were built.

Each of these projects was led by individuals who inspired a team to develop a distinctive work of architecture. Each team creatively interpreted and translated the initial vision into a reality that challenged the idea and thereby made it better. It was their diligence and perseverance in developing and overseeing the work in the field as well as in the office that ultimately led to achieving the quality we sought.

Our exposure to the clients, programs, cultures, and environments we encounter continues to broaden and extend the dimensions of the firm's personality, especially in an ever-shrinking world where cultures increasingly cross-pollinate. Each experience informs some aspect of our body of knowledge and our thought process, often unpredictably, which increasingly inspires us to reach beyond our own limits as individuals and as a firm.

Out of these guiding principles, what has emerged from KPF's rapid ascendancy is a personality that is surprising for a firm of the dimension of this office and for the scale of work undertaken. It is an ethos that recognizes the importance of diligently shepherding the execution of the design intention as much as its creation.

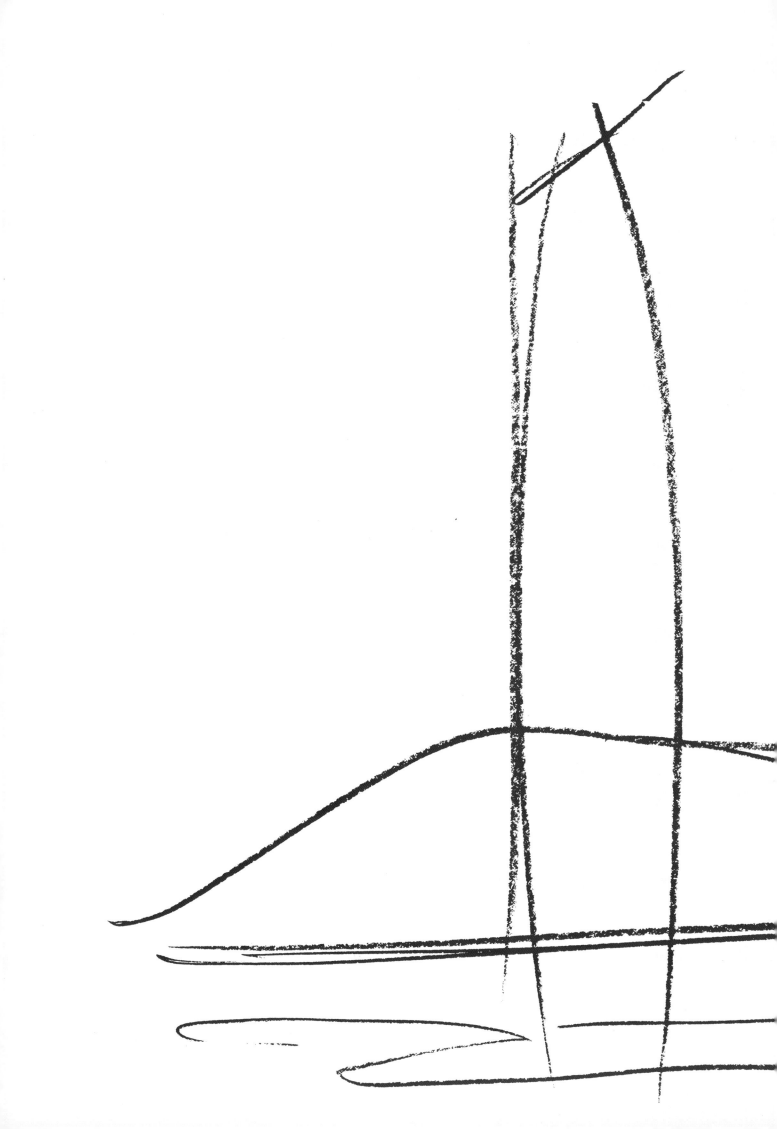

333 Wacker Drive, Chicago

Design/Completion 1979/1983
Chicago, Illinois
Urban Investment & Development Company
1,040,800 square feet
Steel frame, marble, granite, glass, stainless steel
Granite, terrazzo, stainless steel

Designed in 1981, this building creates a
dialogue between figural expression and
abstract expression. In one sense, it can
be viewed as a classical composition of
three parts: base, middle, and top.
Simultaneously, it can be seen as an
abstract composition, the architectural
equivalent of a Brancusi sculpture.

The building is located at a bend in the
Chicago River, on the only triangular site
in Chicago's grid. While monolithic in
volume, it presents two contrasting faces:
one is faceted and addresses the city; the
other is curved and echoes the river's
geometry. The curving face is made more
dynamic by the linear slice carved from
the upper floors. The building's base
is expressed as a weighty mass of stone
rooted to the earth, in contrast to the
lightness of the glass volume above.
Ironically, the building engages its context
by contrasting its sculptural, horizontally-
striated glass body with the massiveness of
the stone buildings that surround it.

William Pedersen

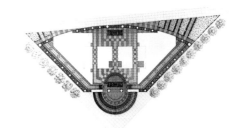

1   Site plan
2   View of base along arcade
3   View from across the Chicago River
4   Base of building on Wacker Drive
5   Base of building on downtown side
6   First floor plan
7   View from elevated train tracks

333 Wacker Drive, Chicago   15

Procter & Gamble General Offices Company Complex

Design/Completion 1982/1985
Cincinnati, Ohio
Procter & Gamble
823,000 square feet
Grey granite, white marble, limestone, dark metal, double-glazed tinted and reflective glass

This new building joins with an existing 1960s structure to form the world headquarters of Procter & Gamble. As an ensemble, the two create a large L-shaped figure focused on an exterior garden.

The buildings are situated on the eastern edge of Cincinnati's downtown core and are therefore required to be both a gateway and a terminus to the city. The duality of this role is exploited by positioning two tower forms at the joint of the L-shaped figure. Externally, they symbolize a gateway to the city. Internally, they focus on and embrace the garden which terminates the eastern edge of the city.

An entry pavilion is introduced as a mediator between garden and building. This structure contains a fountain which becomes the eastern counterpart to the historic Fountain Square in the center of Cincinnati.

The building's limestone cladding connects it to the existing structure, while white marble accentuates the structure, bringing it to a higher visual pitch.

William Pedersen, Alexander Ward

1

2

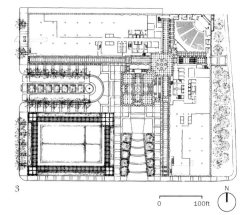

3

0   100ft   N

1   View from northeast towards downtown Cincinnati
2   Aerial view of complex from west
3   First floor plan
4   Dining hall
5   Lobby
6   Light fixture
7   Fountain detail

4

6

5

7

Goldman Sachs European Headquarters, Peterborough Court

Design/Completion 1987/1991
London, England
Goldman Sachs Co.
45,000 square meters
Granite, aluminum, glass
Polished black granite, anigre veneer, glass

Located on Fleet Street, in the heart of the City of London, this building houses a large financial institution. Our role was to make the scale of this structure compatible with the small-scale fragility of its context.

Two axes emerge from an analysis of the site: one is related to Fleet Street and the Old Daily Telegraph Building to which our building is joined; the other represents the grain of the surrounding context.

Reinstating the Old Peterborough Court, we composed our building of pieces which connect to the structure of each of these two grids. The grid of the surrounding context is represented by weighty stone pieces rooted to the earth. The more honorific grid of Fleet Street is addressed by elements of glass—lightweight and hi-tech. The juxtaposition of these two types breaks down the scale of the building into smaller elements and contrasts past and future through the opposition of weight and lightness.

Internally, a glazed ambulatory surrounds the courtyard, which is made brighter by a convex light reflector above.

William Pedersen, Craig Nealy

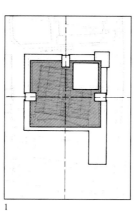

1

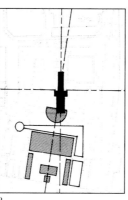

2

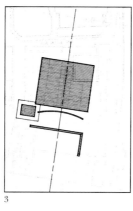

3

4

5

6

7

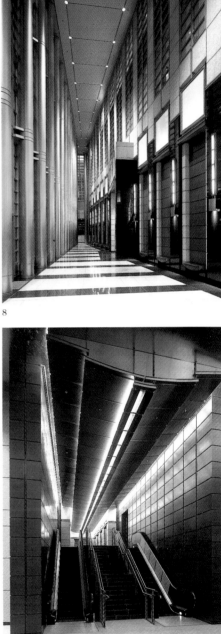

8

9

1 Contextual alignment
2 Fleet Street axis
3 Public spaces
4 Ground floor plan
5 View of south facade from courtyard
6 Aerial view from southwest
7 View of gallery looking toward courtyard
8 Gallery looking west toward cylindrical entry
   volume
9 View from reception hall looking toward elevator
   lobby

10

11

12

10 Cylindrical volume at west entry
11 View from southwest across the Thames River
12 Semi-circular reception area
13 Second floor plan (trading)
14 Seventh–Ninth floor plan (offices)
15 10th floor plan (dining)
Opposite:
  Courtyard separating new structure from reclad
  existing structure

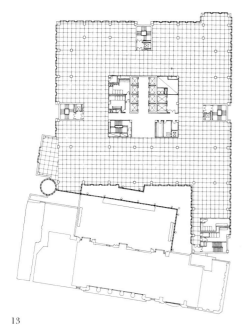

13

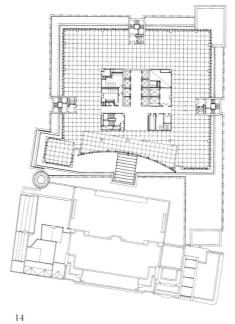

14

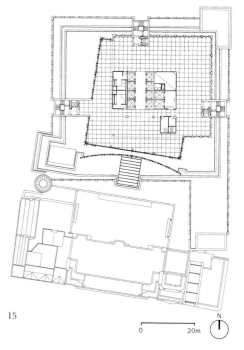

15

0   20m   N

Westend Str. 1/DG Bank Headquarters

Design/Completion 1986/1993
Frankfurt am Main, Germany
AGIMA/DG Immobilien Anlagegesellschaft mbH
57,000 square meters (office tower)
20,000 square meters (office low-rise)
Granite, aluminum, glass, steel plate (crown)

Located along the famous Mainzer Landstrasse in Frankfurt, this site faces south to a commercial/retail sector and north to an adjacent residential community. Our building strives to acknowledge and represent this duality.

The urban juxtaposition of this site inspired a new composition for the tall building: a composition of three parts. Of these, the two external parts respond to the commercial–residential dialogue. These parts are intended to oppose each other. The third part represents the internal core biology of the building. Like a skewer, it joins the two extroverted parts.

The tension inherent in this opposition is heightened by rendering one part in stone and the other in glass. The rectangular stone volume faces the residential neighborhood and rises to a height of 150 meters (492 feet). This was the limiting height for tall buildings until 1989 and is clearly marked as an urban datum on Frankfurt's skyline. The second volume is curved and rendered in glass. It addresses the commercial context and the Main River and gestures to the center

Continued

1

2

1 Site plan
2 View from the Westend residential district
(northeast)
3 Typical low-rise floor plan
4 Typical high-rise floor plan
5 Ground floor plan
6 Second floor plan
7 Entrance to the winter garden, looking northeast
at night
8 The interior of the winter garden, a public space,
bathed in daylight
9 South elevation of the tower and winter garden
10 East elevation of the high- and low-rise office
complex

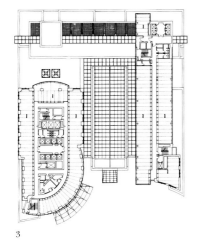

3

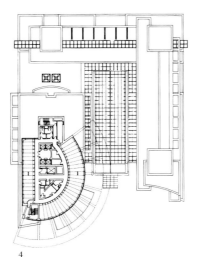

4

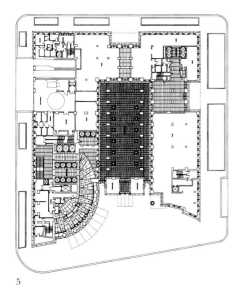

5

6

0   20m

N

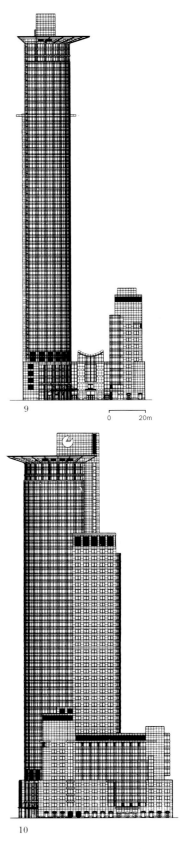

9

0   20m

7

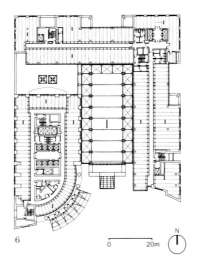

8

10

of the old city of Frankfurt. It is
terminated by a projecting cornice-fan
which is intended to magnify the spatial
quality of this gesture and also to convey
a sense of "roof" to the plaza below.

This building is the first of three tall
structures we have designed which employ
a three-part composition as a method of
establishing urban connections for a tall
building. The other two buildings are 1250
René-Lévesque in Montreal (featured on
page 28) and Rockefeller Plaza West in
New York (featured on page 32). This
strategy of composition exploits the
possibilities of urban juxtaposition that are
inherent in tall buildings. Opposites such
as heavy–light, formal–informal, static–
dynamic and even male–female are
intended to be read and resolved
in the structure's composition.

William Pedersen, Paul King

11

12

13

11   View from the Westend
12   View from across the Main River
13   South facade
14   View from the train station
15   West facade
16   Main entrance
17   Northeast facade

14

15

16

17

18

19

20

18   The landmark on the skyline
19   A magnificent presence on Mainzer Landstrasse
20   Blending into the context of the Westend
Opposite:
      Entrance to the winter garden

1250 Boulevard René-Lévesque/
IBM Quebec Headquarters

Design/Completion 1988/1992
Montreal, Canada
Marathon Realty & IBM Canada, Ltd
111,482 square meters
Granite, glass, aluminum, steel
Granite, marble, anigre veneer, stainless steel, glass, plaster

Designed as the Canadian headquarters of the IBM Corporation, this building strives to represent the spirit of advanced technology.

The site is at the edge of Montreal's existing downtown core, adjacent to Winsor Station. Our strategy seeks to dramatize the boundary between two precincts: the city center and its surrounding context. This is accomplished by positioning the main structure against the outer boundary of the site, creating a large "urban room" facing towards the city. The edges of this room are animated by a pergola structure, a curved office entry, and a winter garden.

Above, the building extends this sense of boundary by the juxtaposition of a rectangular stone edge facing outwards and a curved glass form facing inwards, towards the city and the cathedral. The stone surfaces are vertically striated with a sub-rhythm of horizontal mullions. The curved glass surfaces extend these horizontal mullions into a full-blown lateral stratification, creating a weave of horizontals and verticals.

Continued

1

2

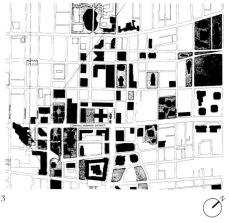

3

1   View across church
2   View across Boulevard René-Lévesque
3   Urban context plan
4   View from cathedral
5   View of entry plaza
6   View of entry plaza at night
7   43rd–45th floor plan
8   Fifth–Sixth floor plan
9   Mezzanine floor plan
10 Restaurant floor plan
11 Ground floor plan

4

5

6

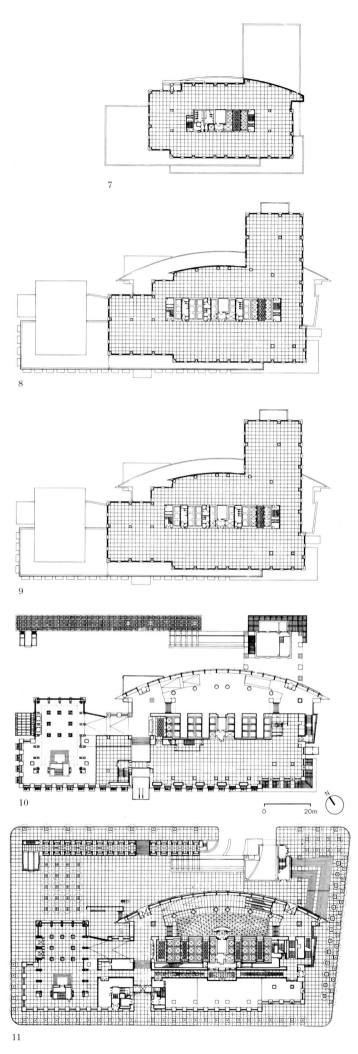

7

8

9

10

0   20m

11

From a distance, the building reveals itself as a dynamic interplay of volumes. However, at the building's base, these same elements are more symmetrically composed, establishing a smaller scale that relates to the human body. Thus, the building achieves an equilibrium between stasis and thrust.

William Pedersen, John Koga, Richard Clarke

12 View from Winsor Station
13 Entry step from Winsor Station
14 Office lobby
15 Pergola on courtyard
16 Office entrance
17 Winter garden

12

13

14

15

16

17

Rockefeller Plaza West

Design/Completion 1987/1991
New York, New York
Rockefeller Center Development Corporation
1,600,000 square feet
Structural steel, limestone, granite, glass curtainwall, metal
Marble, terrazzo, metal

This building is envisioned to be the western gateway to Rockefeller Center. Its site, at the northern boundary of the Times Square district, requires that it create a dialogue not only with Rockefeller Center, but also with Times Square— a type of "Janus" structure which speaks to both worlds.

Inspired by the Rockefeller G.E. Building, our layered composition unfolds around a central core as it rises to a similar height, visually connecting the two buildings along an east–west axis. While the G.E. Building is layered in a symmetrical composition Rockefeller Plaza West is layered asymmetrically. This De Stijl-like composition allows the east–west energy generated from the heart of Rockefeller Center to be redirected to a north–south axis, connecting it with Times Square.

The building is composed of elements from these two worlds. Mostly clad in vertically-striated limestone, as is Rockefeller Center, our building incorporates signage and iconographic pieces drawn from the spirit of Times Square.

William Pedersen, Paul Gates, Kevin Kennon

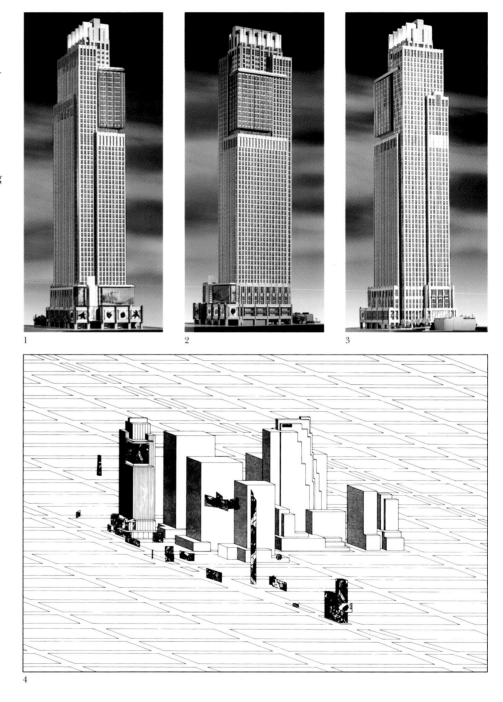

1

2

3

4

1   Northwest elevation
2   Southwest elevation
3   Southeast elevation
4   Urban context axonometric at Rockefeller
    Center and Times Square
5   7th Avenue elevation
6   49th Street elevation
7   East elevation facing Rockefeller Plaza

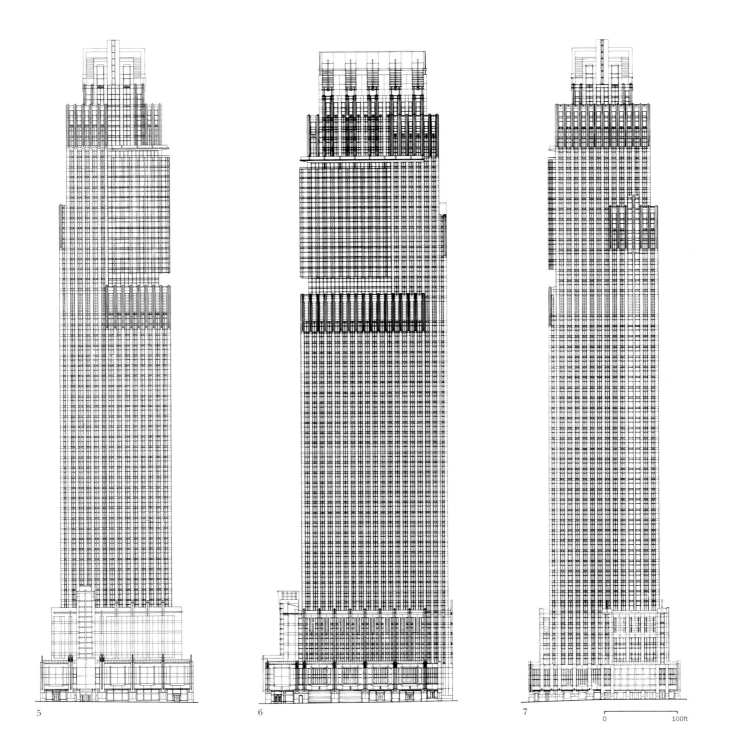

5   6   7

0   100ft

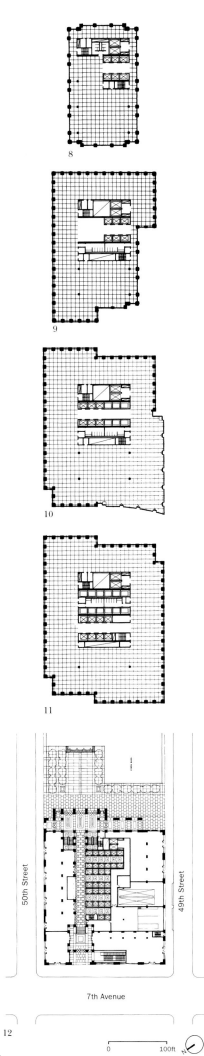

8

9

10

11

13

14

15

50th Street

49th Street

7th Avenue

12

0   100ft   N

8   56th–57th floor plan
9   52nd–55th floor plan
10 40th–45th floor plan
11 Eighth–36th floor plan
12 Ground floor plan
13 Central lobby looking west
14 Concierge desk
15 West lobby
16 Urban context view from southwest
17 Base at plaza and 50th Street corner
18 Base at 7th Avenue
19 Base at 50th Street

16

17

18

19

Newport Harbor Art Museum

Design/Completion 1990/1991
Newport Beach, California
Newport Harbor Art Museum
75,000 square feet
Concrete, stucco, stone, lead-coated copper
Plaster, stone, wood

This museum seeks to join art, landscape, and light in a singular composition. Exterior courtyards become the dominant vehicle for this linkage.

Here we have created a fabric of spaces, some internal and some external. These spaces are united by a curved circulation gallery which binds together the separate parts.

Natural light dominates the quality of the internal rooms. The characteristics of this light have been modulated to achieve a distinctly different quality for each room. The external courtyards similarly strive for unique character: each space has been landscaped to serve as a backdrop for the art positioned within the adjacent rooms. Some introduce water as an acoustic element, while others exploit it for its luminosity.

The entire structure is to be clad in stucco on concrete with wood doors and window frames. The stucco is to be textured and painted to emphasize the uniqueness of each room.

William Pedersen, Paul Katz, Joshua Chaiken

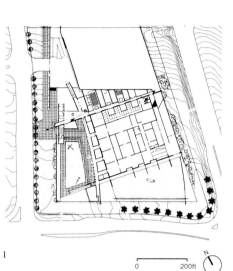

1

2

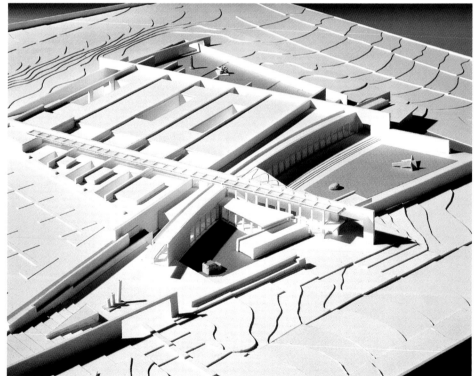

3

1 Gallery level plan
2 Roof plan
3 View from north with car drop-off in foreground
4 West elevation
5 South elevation
6 East elevation
7 View from west showing reflecting pool in center and sculpture court on right
8 View from south with reflecting pool in foreground
9 Phase I site plan
10 Phase II site plan

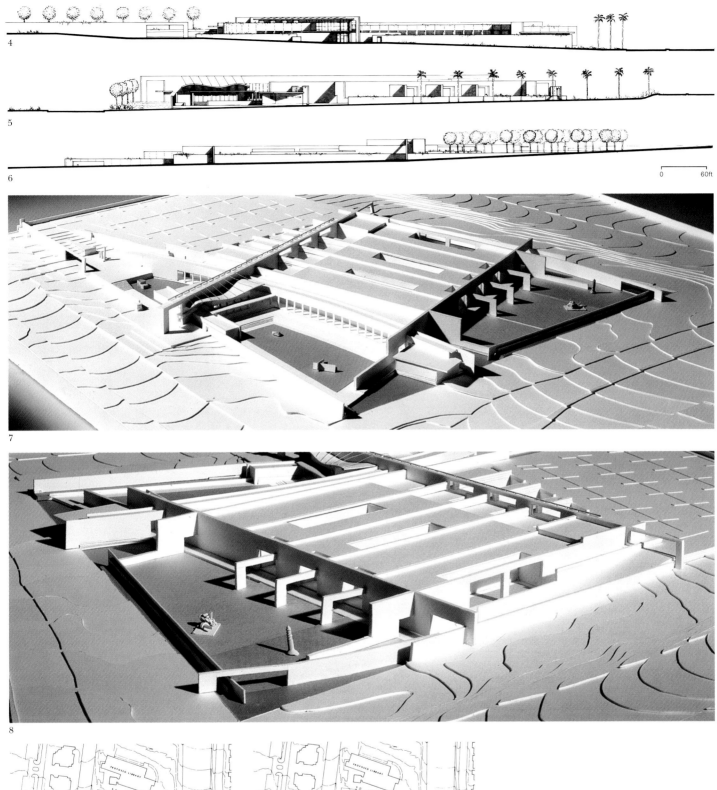

4

5

6

0   60ft

7

8

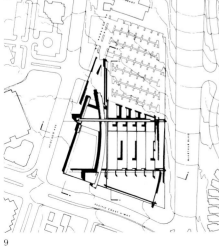

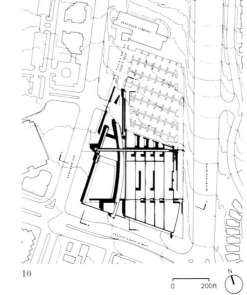

9   10

0   200ft   N

Carwill House II

Design/Completion 1989/1991
Stratton, Vermont
Private residence
6,500 square feet
Wooden frame, lead-coated copper, cedar, slate
Slate, plaster, wood

This is a house designed for the mountains. Our intention was to create a dwelling which both grew from and was juxtaposed against its site. A steep rocky slope sponsors the dynamics of this structure, which faces south to Stratton Mountain in Vermont.

Long tendon-like forms are created to frame a fissure cut into the rock, shaping an entry court. These linear forms, which contain bedrooms and other functions, join a living room and dining room of curvilinear geometry. In turn, both of these are linked to a cylindrical tower which pins together the total composition.

The house is clad in a tripartite organization: a base of cubic slate; walls of rough-sawn cedar planks bolted to the wooden frame; and roofs of lead-coated copper. Internally, spaces infused with natural light express the full potential of this complex geometry.

William Pedersen, Joshua Chaiken

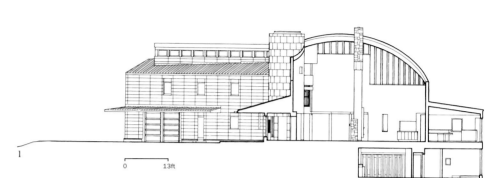

1

0   13ft

2

38

3

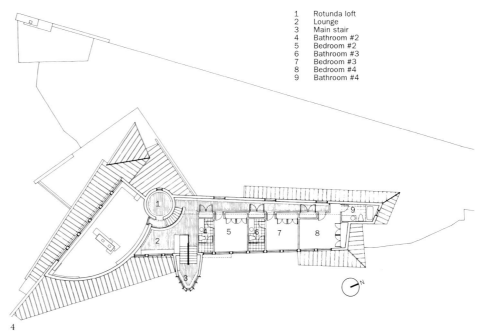

4

1	Rotunda loft
2	Lounge
3	Main stair
4	Bathroom #2
5	Bedroom #2
6	Bathroom #3
7	Bedroom #3
8	Bedroom #4
9	Bathroom #4

5

6

0   40ft

7

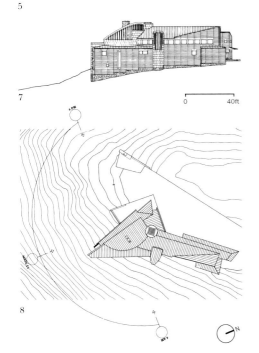

8

9

10

1 Section through living/dining room
2 View from southwest
3 View from southeast
4 Entry level plan
5 View from top of main stair
6 View from west
7 East elevation
8 Site plan
9 Living room clerestory
10 Detail view of east elevation

Federal Reserve Bank of Dallas

Design/Completion 1989/1992
Dallas, Texas
Federal Reserve Bank of Dallas
1,050,000 square feet
Reinforced concrete, steel, limestone, aluminum, glass
Granite, travertine, stainless steel, bronze, wood

Here we attempt to express the dignity and stability of federal government using the language of Modern architecture. Positioned across the Woodall Expressway, this building looks towards the city of Dallas and specifically its arts district. From this context we selected the two dominant but related axes of Pearl Street and the expressway as the basis of our composition.

The building is composed of three dominant parts. The first is made up of the vaults and articulations related to money processing. The second contains public spaces such as dining areas, training facilities, and the auditorium. The third comprises office space, including large areas for maximum flexibility and smaller areas for executive functions. This tripartite composition forms the building's vertical section.

The heart of our structure is a courtyard containing a central garden. This garden joins all of the functions of the building and connects them into an ensemble, encouraging a sense of community.

Continued

1

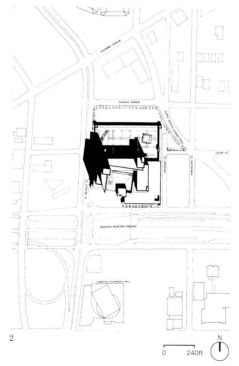

2

0   240ft   N

3

1   View from expressway
2   Site plan
3   Detail of tower
4   View of dining pavilion
5   View to city
6   View from southwest
7   Office plan

4

5

6

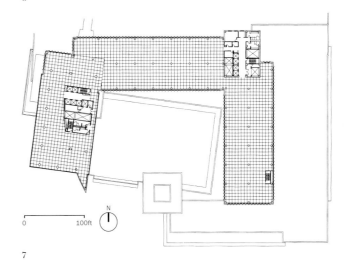

7

Spiraling around the garden are a series of masses which gradually ascend to a tower housing the executive functions.

The building is clad primarily in limestone, similar to that of the adjacent Meyerson Concert Hall. The stone surfaces are countered by glass elements which punctuate the structure, emphasizing important functions.

William Pedersen, Richard Clarke

10

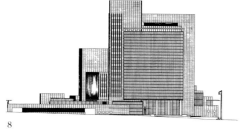

8

0   100ft

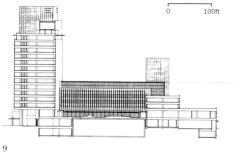

9

8   West elevation
9   Transverse section
10   Detail of tower
11   Interior of lobby
12   Detail of lobby
13   View from northwest
14   Main entrance

11

12

13

14

World Bank Headquarters

Design/Completion 1989/1997
Washington, DC
International Bank for Reconstruction & Development
1,200,000 square feet
Precast and cast-in-place concrete curtainwall, clear and reflective
insulating glass units
Painted aluminum, resinous stone, painted steel, epoxy terrazo
with glass aggregate

The World Bank serves all nations of the
world, in particular those with developing
economies. Hence, this building eschews
the Classical language of Washington's
governmental buildings in favor of the
more universal language of contemporary
Modernism.

Our design builds upon two of the World
Bank's existing structures (both from the
1960s) and uses them to initiate a new
context. Staged construction led to the
choice of completing a pinwheel
composition generated by the two existing
buildings. A primary product of this
composition is a great cubic room,
150 feet wide by 150 feet high, which
is symbolic of the World Bank's mission.
Expressing the community of nations, it
joins together all of the Bank's functions
and its members. Flooded in natural light,
this central space becomes the internal
equivalent of a town square. Its character
is generated by the inclusion of various
elements which represent, abstractly,
icons of world architecture. Light and
water dominate this space.

Continued

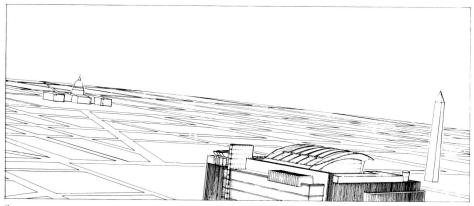

1

2

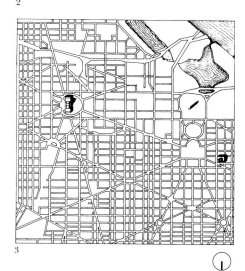

3

1 Overall view from northeast
2 Site diagram
3 Site plan
4 Entry on Pennsylvania Avenue
5 Curtainwall detail
6 East elevation
7 South elevation
8 West elevation
9 North elevation

N

4

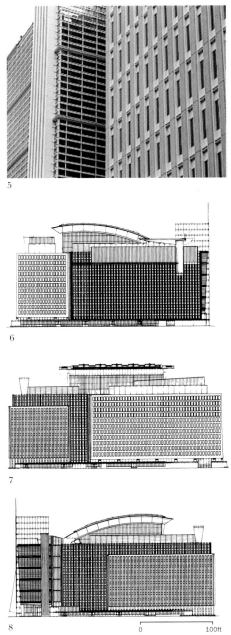

5

6

7

8

0   100ft

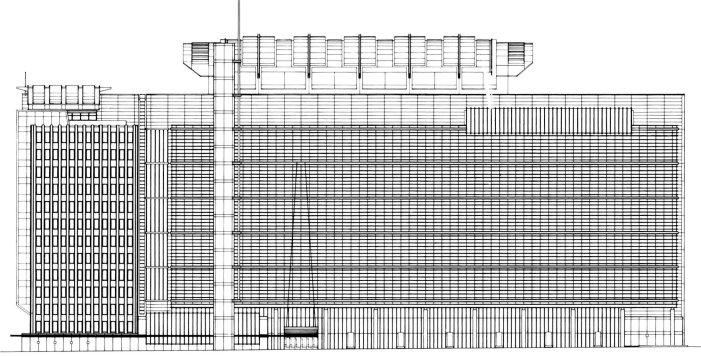

9

0   50ft

10

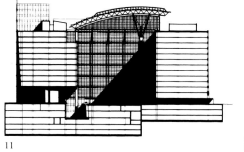

11

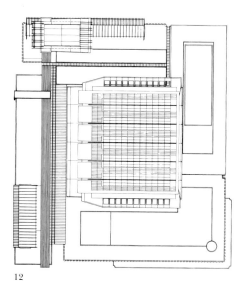

12

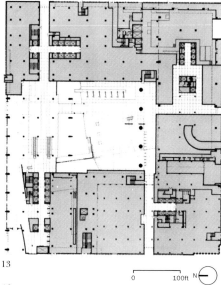

13

Externally, the building creates a dialogue between pieces of great weight and those of lightness. Raised three stories over an entry lobby, the horizontally striated glass facade along Pennsylvania Avenue offers a view into the heart of the Bank's central room, its transparency encouraging access to the building. Countering this gesture are the vertically striated concrete walls which derive from, and connect to, the existing structures. Old and new are brought together into a single entity.

William Pedersen, Craig Nealy

10   Atrium
11   North–south section
12   Roof plan
13   Ground floor plan
14   Monumental stair off atrium
Opposite:
     Conference tower

14

0   100ft   N

16

17

18

19

20

21

23

22

24

16   View of atrium from dining terrace
17   Atrium
18   Water trough in atrium
19   Bridges at lobby and cafeteria levels with
     reflecting pool below
20   Executive director's conference room and
     lounge
21   Typical office corridor
22&23 Executive director's boardroom
24   Boardroom table detail

First Hawaiian Center

Design/Completion 1991/1995
Honolulu, Hawaii
First Hawaiian Bank
600,000 square feet
Limestone and glass curtainwall

Hawaii is memorable for its landscape:
the dramatic confrontation between
the mountains and the sea is profound.
The tension in this dynamic landscape
of juxtapositions inspired a unique
architectural language for a Honolulu
skyscraper.

The tower is composed of two distinct
forms, one which faces the sea and the
other which faces the mountains, linked
to the ground by a low podium containing
a museum and a banking hall. This
podium engages the tower with the urban
context and shapes a series of gardens
along the surrounding streets.

The building's fenestration codifies each
of its major parts: horizontally louvered
windows frame views of the sea and the
horizon; vertically proportioned

Continued

1

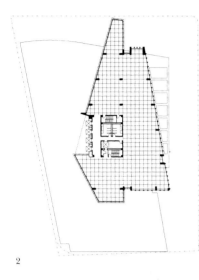

2

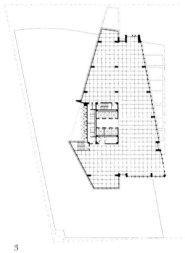

3

5

6

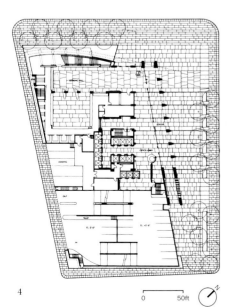

4

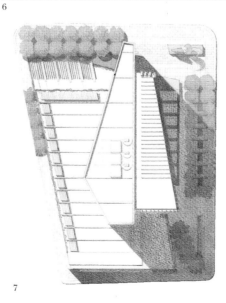

7

1 Main entrance
2 Typical high-rise floor plan
3 Typical low-rise floor plan
4 Ground floor plan
5 Entrance canopy
6 Art wall of museum
7 Site plan

0   50ft

fenestration faces the mountains; and the podium is dominated by a great wall of prismatic-glass louvers. These louvers fracture the light passing through them into a dazzling spectral brilliance. This kaleidoscopic display of natural light continually transforms the interior of the museum and the banking hall.

Peter Schubert, William Pedersen

8

9

8   Museum art wall by day
9   Museum art wall by night
10   Front elevation
11   View from ocean
12   View from park and mountains
13   Aerial view of terrace

10

11

12

13

14

15

16

17

18

19

20

21

22

23

24

14   View of entry canopy from garden
15   View at ocean facade
16   Museum/banking hall
17   Museum/banking hall stairs
18   Banking hall
19   Trust department conference room
20   Beneath stair in museum/banking hall
21   Curtainwall detail
22   Museum/banking hall
23   View of garden with fountain
24   View along street facade

US Courthouse, Portland

Design/Completion 1992/1997
Portland, Oregon
General Services Administration
602,000 square feet
Indiana limestone, jet mist granite, stainless steel, aluminum,
reflective glass

The modern, 21st century United States Federal Courthouse is composed of two dominant programmatic elements: the courts, and those agencies that serve the courts. Hence, a single structure serves both the judicial and the bureaucratic functions. The duality of this mission lies at the heart of the architectural order of the building.

Fundamental also is our desire for the building to "explain" its function. We believe that the judicial process needs to be visually understood, reinforcing the civic role of the courts building. Therefore, each of the various functional components is given a specific representation. Unifying the diversity of these components in the exterior expression was our greatest challenge.

In general, the parts which contain the courtroom elements are made weighty.

Continued

1

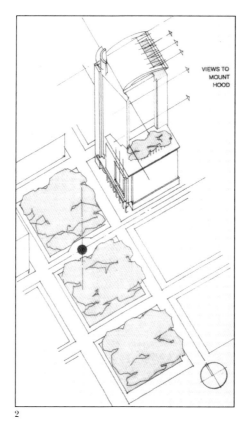

2

3

1   Site location
2   Contextual influences
3   View of downtown and Mount Hood from Vista Bridge
4   View from northwest

56

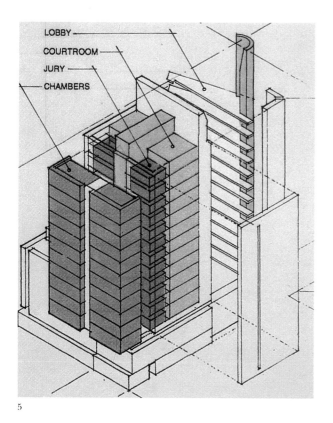

LOBBY
COURTROOM
JURY
CHAMBERS

5

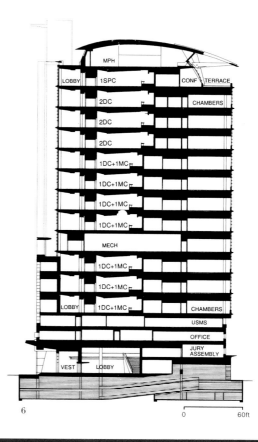

	MPH		
LOBBY	1SPC	CONF	TERRACE
	2DC		CHAMBERS
	2DC		
	2DC		
	1DC+1MC		
	1DC+1MC		
	1DC+1MC		
	1DC+1MC		
	MECH		
	1DC+1MC		
	1DC+1MC		
LOBBY	1DC+1MC		CHAMBERS
			USMS
			OFFICE
			JURY ASSEMBLY
VEST	LOBBY		

6

0   60ft

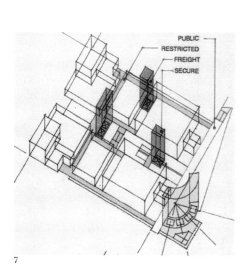

PUBLIC
RESTRICTED
FREIGHT
SECURE

7

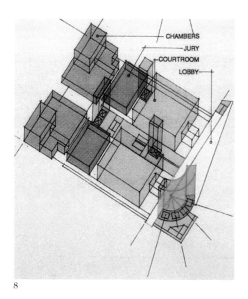

CHAMBERS
JURY
COURTROOM
LOBBY

8

9

Those that interact with the courtrooms—the judges' chambers and public circulation galleries—are made light. The dialogue between lightness and weight is this building's most significant aesthetic.

External pressures generated by the site are acknowledged in the building's forms; in particular, the vertical tower which bounds the northern edge of the park, the glass wall of the public galleries which deflects to the center of the park, and the sail-like roof gesturing to the Willamette River and Mount Hood in the distance.

William Pedersen, Jerri Smith

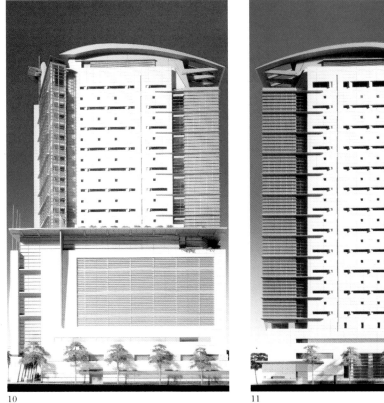

10

11

5   Organizational diagram
6   Building section
7&8   Organizational diagram
9   View from east
10   South facade
11   North facade
12   View from southwest

12

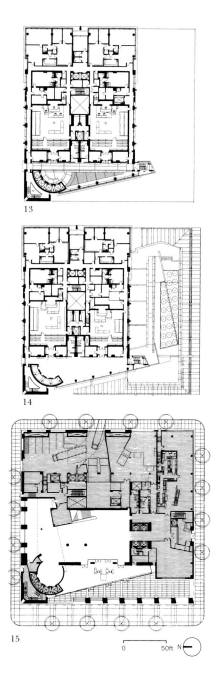

13

14

15

16

17

0   50ft N

13 Typical courts floor plan
14 Ninth floor plan showing eighth floor terrace
15 Ground floor plan
16 Crown at courtroom lobbies
17 Terrace at eighth floor
18 Roof trellis at 16th floor terrace
19 Light scoops diagram
20 View from Hawthorne Bridge

18

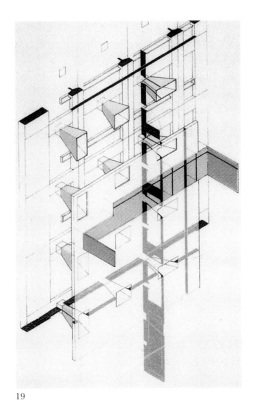

19

20

Aid Association for Lutherans, Headquarters Expansion

Design/Completion 1993/1995
Appleton, Wisconsin
Aid Association for Lutherans
500,000 square feet
White aluminum plate

William Pedersen designed this building in the early 1970s, while in the office of John Carl Warnecke and Associates. With this project he introduced a design strategy based upon structured duality which has been central to his work for the past 25 years.

This building is dominated by themes related to the man–nature dialogue: it rests lightly on the earth; nature passes through the building rather than surrounding it; and natural light, ever changing in quality and intensity, infuses all the working spaces. Rectangular geometries (man-made) and circular geometries (from nature) interact. The circular geometries express spaces of gathering and community, while the rectangular geometries are associated with private working areas.

Continued

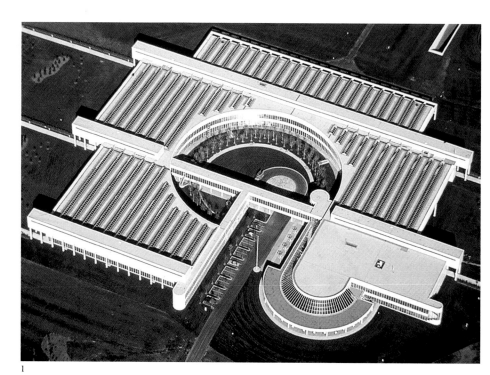

1

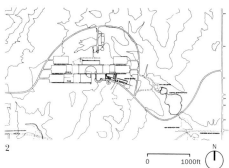

2

3

4

5

1 Headquarters building prior to expansion
2 Site plan
3 Headquarters building; north elevation
4&5 Headquarters building; elevation details of
    expansion
6 Headquarters building with expansion; south
    elevation

6

KPF's recent expansion of the building accommodates a new entry lobby to handle greatly increased visitor requirements, executive private office space, and an auditorium function. Its character is an outgrowth of the original building, and it attempts to heighten the meaning of pre-existing themes.

William Pedersen

7

8

9

10

11

12

Greater Buffalo International Airport

Design/Completion 1993/1997
Buffalo, New York
Niagara Frontier Transportation Authority
285,000 square feet
Steel, metal cladding, glass

Experiencing the ground–air relationship is a fundamental sensation of flight. This relationship can be thought of as heavy versus light, static versus dynamic, or solid versus void. Our design attempts to give physical representation to these basic dualities. Additionally, we intended that this structure represent a gateway or passage into and out of the Niagara Frontier region.

Three dominant parts define our structure: the arrival/departure hall, the concessions link, and the concourse. We intended to give specific form to each of these experiences and to articulate these as separate, but connected, episodes in a procession to and from the aircraft.

Of these three, the dominant component is the arrival/departure hall. Its form sets the theme for the structure and is a direct representation of the ground–air dialogue central to the nature of flight. Two long parallel curving walls form the north and

Continued

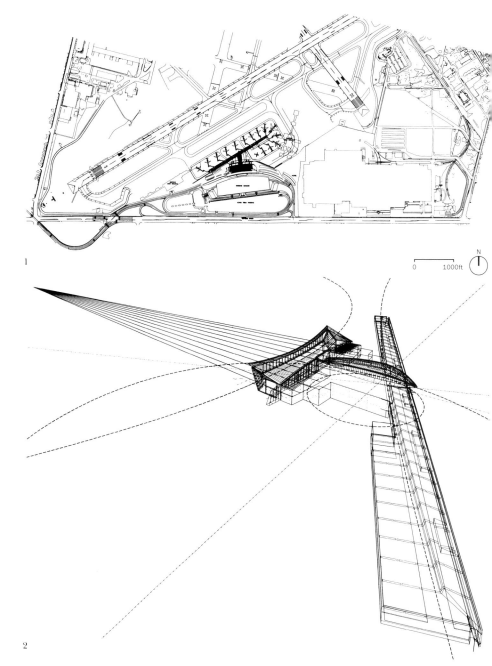

1

0   1000ft   N

2

1   Site plan
2   Building geometry
3   Plan of the departure level
4   Building axonometry
5   Ticketing hall interior, looking north
6   View from the concessions area toward the main
    entrance

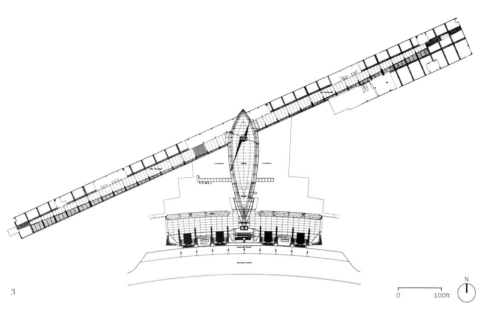

3

south boundaries of this room. The north wall separates the arrivals area from the concessions link. The south wall faces the city and incorporates the building's main entry.

The north wall is massive and is formed as a gently curving concrete arch. Penetrations through it are intended to be experienced as movement through a gate-like structure. The south wall is light and shaped in the form of a wing in flight. Composed of metal and glass, it soars while the other stands planted heavily on the earth. These two opposing surfaces are connected by straight beam segments, generating the spatial volume and bringing equilibrium to the dialogue of apparently opposing parts.

William Pedersen, Duncan Reid

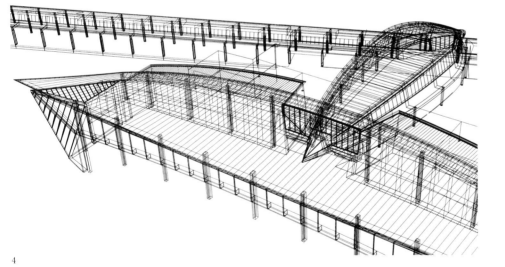

4

5   6

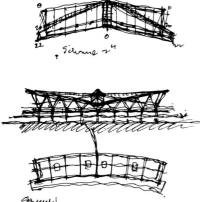

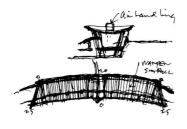

8

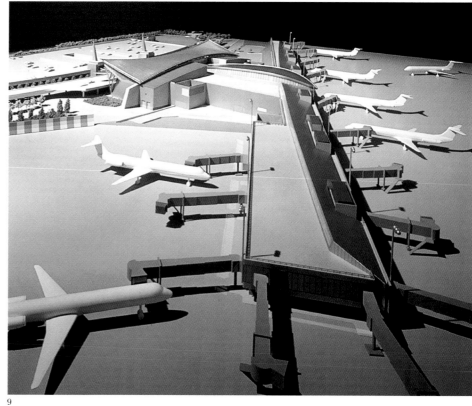

7

9

10

7   Schematic sketches
8   Three-level parking garage fronting the ticketing hall
9   Aerial view of the entire project from the northeast
10 Eastern approach to the main terminal
11 Aerial view
12 Warped metal roof studies

11

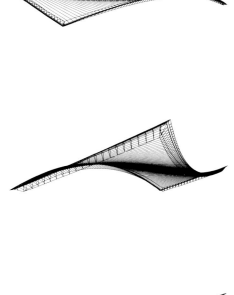

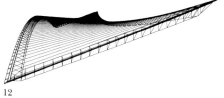

12

Dacom Headquarters Building

Design/Completion 1995/1999
Seoul, Korea
Dacom Corporation
347 square meters (site area)
5,879 square meters (building area)
Building area: 63,473.34 square feet
Glass, aluminum, granite

As with 333 Wacker Drive in Chicago, we attempted to create a composition which is both figural and abstract. The sculptured simplicity gains strength from its contrast with the visually chaotic surroundings.

Located on the northern edge of the Han River, this site serves as a gateway at the end of the Han Gang Bridge. We responded to this context with a prismatic-faceted wall of a scale which firmly marks an important presence for Dacom in the surrounding community. This wall initiates a spiral composition terminating in a communications mast, which becomes a symbolic and literal icon of the company's corporate identity.

Continued

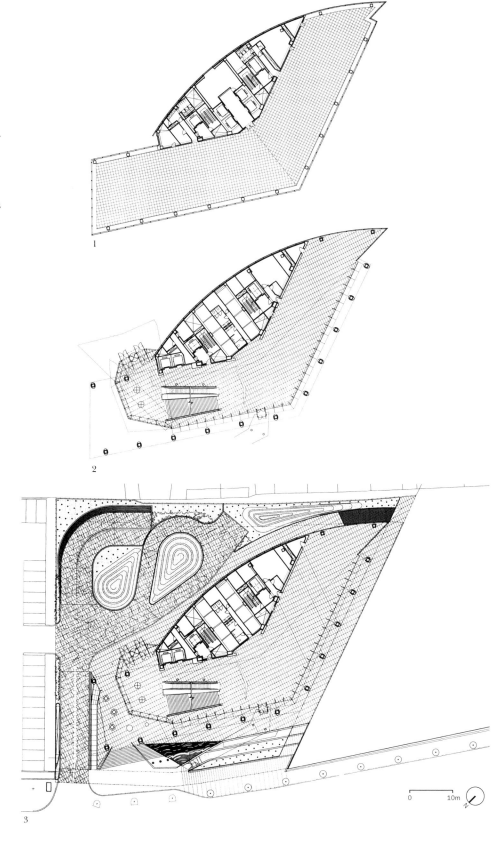

1   Typical high-rise floor plan
2   Ground floor plan
3   Site plan
4   The gentle elegance of the curved east facade

One approaches the building through a serene garden and motor court. At the entry point, we introduce architectural elements of increasing complexity and texture. A series of canopies and screen walls counter the smoothness of the building's green-tinted glass body. The building's base and entry point generate a human scale which complements the adjacent garden.

William Pedersen, John Koga

5

6

5 The straight and curved forms embrace in a spiraling mass

6 The west facade gives every office a view to the river

7 The new headquarters viewed from the existing Dacom building

8 The north edge hides the unusual geometry of the building

9 The south edge of the building as seen from across the river, on the highway leading to the city center

10 View of the main drop-off and entrance under the dramatic canopy

11 The office lobby is raised to allow better views of the river

7

8

9

10

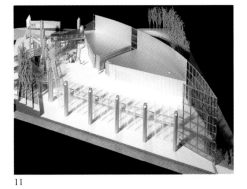

11

Shanghai World Financial Center

Design/Completion 1994/2002
Shanghai, China
Mori Building Co. Ltd
317,000 square meters (total)
240,000 square meters (above grade)
Smooth and rough granite (tower base), horizontally banded
stainless steel, lightly reflective glass (tower shaft)

The ancient Chinese conceived of the earth as a square and the sky as a circle. The interaction between these two geometric forms gives rise to the physical form and structure of this tower. It also endows the tower with a cultural and cosmological resonance which establishes it as a powerful icon.

The Chinese government has designated the Pudong area of Shanghai as a massive development zone, successfully attracting foreign investment. Our intention is to counter the inevitable visual cacophony that will emerge from this growth with a structure of great simplicity. The building's two dominant functions—office and hotel—each require specific floor plates. Our goal is to provide both within an elemental, monolithic form.

The primary shape of the tower is devised as an extruded square intersected by two sweeping arcs, tapering to a single line at its top. A square prism and a cylinder intersect to create the building's physical form. The gradual progression of floor

Continued

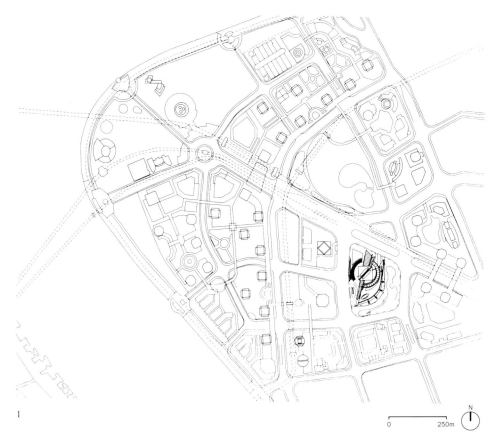

1

0   250m

2

74

plans generates configurations which are ideal for offices on the lower floors and hotel suites above. At the same time, the transformation of the plan rotates the orientation of the tower by 45 degrees, aligning the tower top with the Oriental Pearl TV Tower, Pudong's dominant landmark. To relieve wind pressure at the top of our structure we carved out a 50-meter (164-foot) cylindrical void, equal in diameter to the "pearl" sphere of the TV tower. The solid–void dialogue created by this relationship further connects these two structures.

Penetrating through and surrounding the massive stone base of the tower are wall, wing, and conical forms. The varied geometries of these functional elements express the procession of the entry sequence into the building. The clustering of smaller forms at the ground plane introduces a human scale and expresses the complexities of pedestrian movement, complementing the simplicity of the tower.

William Pedersen, Joshua Chaiken

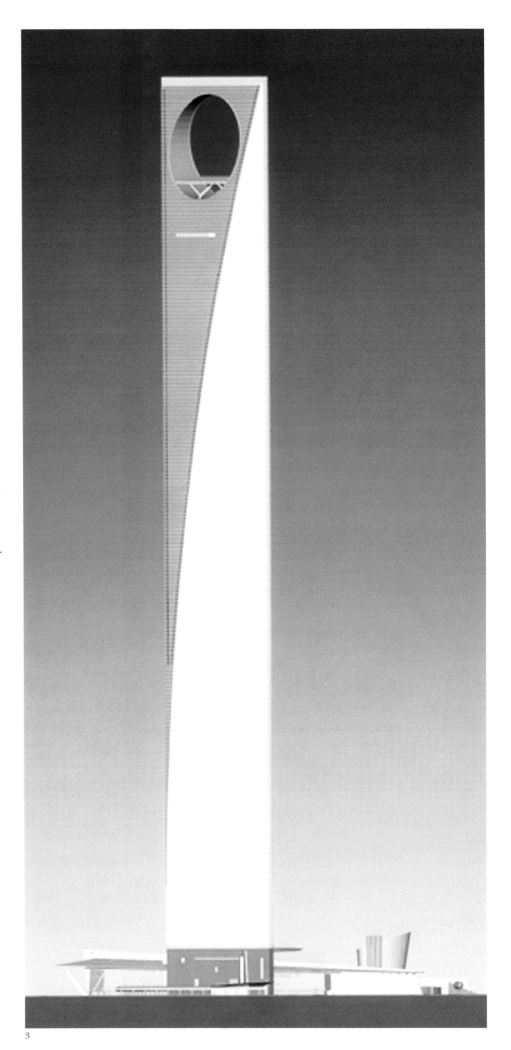

3

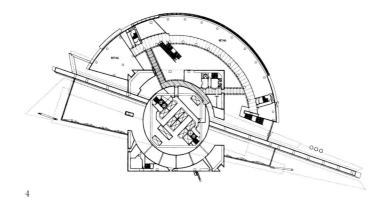

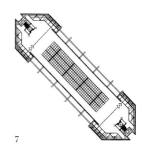

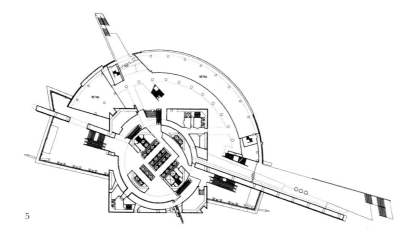

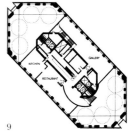

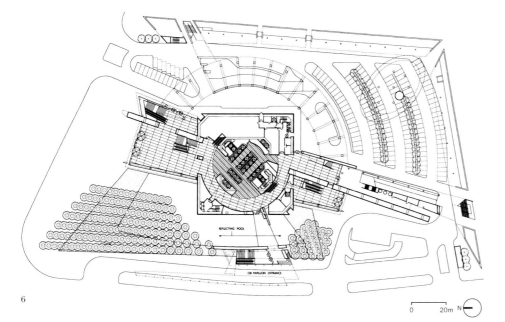

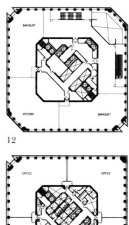

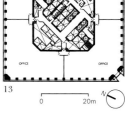

0   20m   N

4   Third floor plan
5   Second floor plan
6   First floor plan
7   Observation bridge
8   Observation deck: bridge elevator access
9   Observation deck: restaurant and gallery
10   Hotel guest room
11   Typical hotel guestroom floor
12   Hotel reception floor
13   Typical office floor
14   Tower section
15   Southwest elevation

0   20m   N

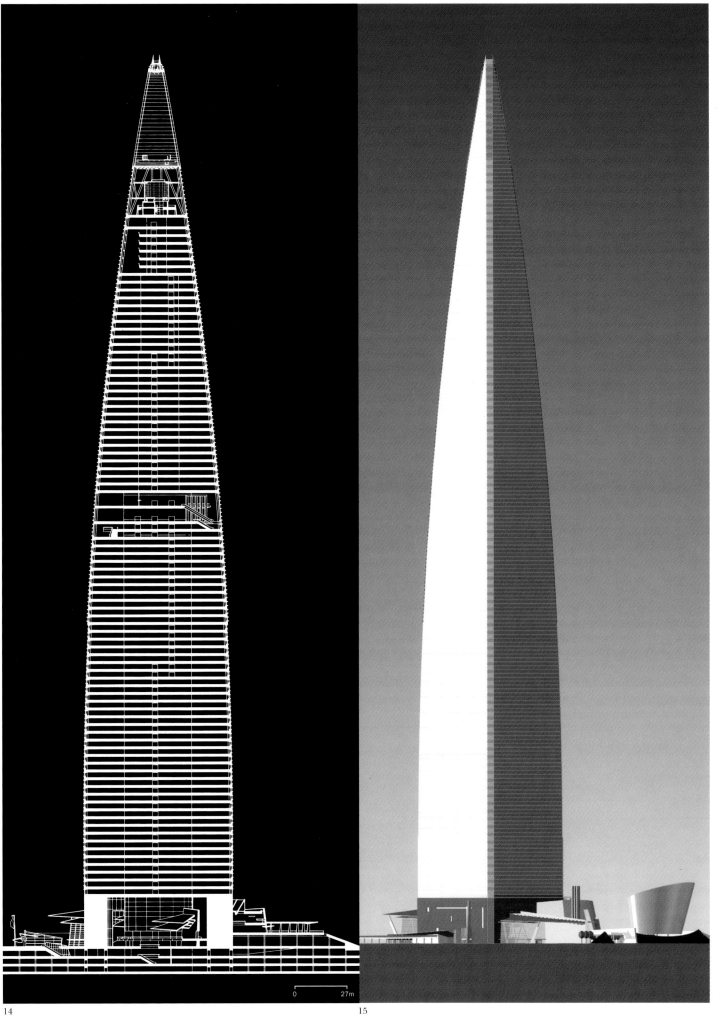

14

15

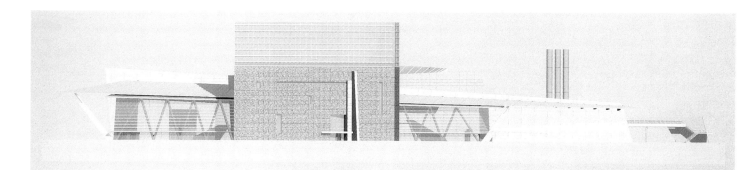

16

17

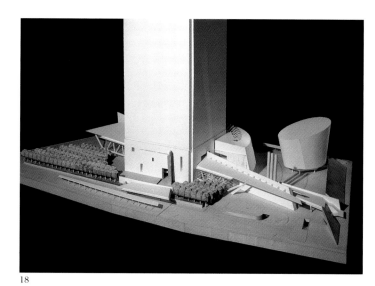

18

16   Podium: west elevation
17&18   Podium: study model
19   Podium: east elevation
20&21   Podium: study model
22&23   Office lobby entrance: study model

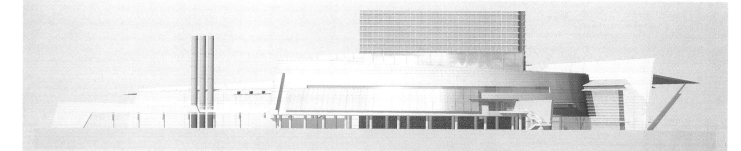

19

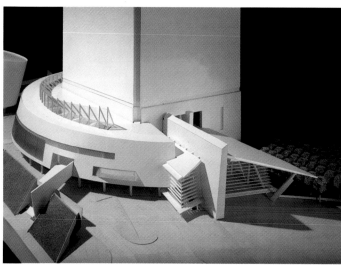

20

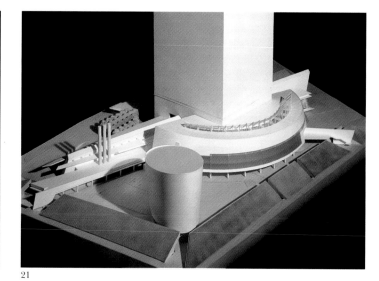

21

22

23

SBS Competition

Competition 1995
Seoul, Korea
Seoul Broadcasting System
84,120 square meters
Stainless steel roof, glass curtainwall, aluminum panels

This building for the Seoul Broadcasting System (SBS) is composed of large studio spaces and other support facilities of a more general nature. The clear duality of these functions inspires the building's composition.

Broadcasting creates waves which emanate from a central point. The circular geometry of such a wave pattern suggests one aspect of our building's form. The flexibility required of the studios, however, demands an orthogonal form.

The juxtaposition of these two geometric types, the orthogonal and the circular, generates the building's shape. Heightening this contrast is the combination of long-span, multi-story structure for the studio spaces and short-span structure for the surrounding office space. A tall void separates the two spatial types and becomes the heart of the building's interior.

Externally, the building spirals about the volume of the studio spaces. These spaces are terminated by a great community roof-garden room, for dining and lectures, sheltered by a south-facing glass enclosure.

William Pedersen, Duncan Reid

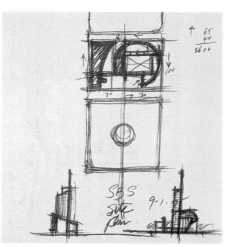

1

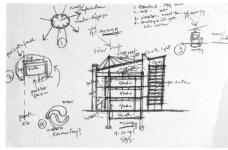

2

3

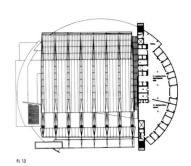

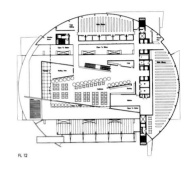

FL 13

FL 12

FL 11

0   30m

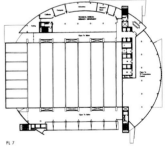

FL 7

4

0   30m

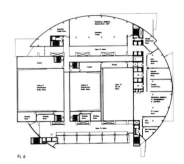

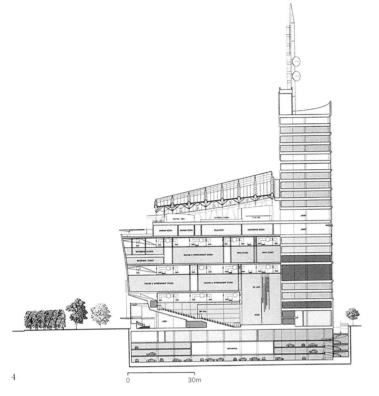

FL 6

5

N

0   30m

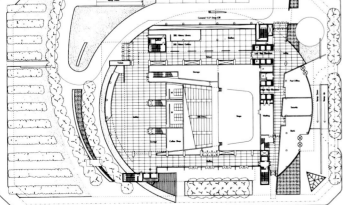

7

FL 5

6

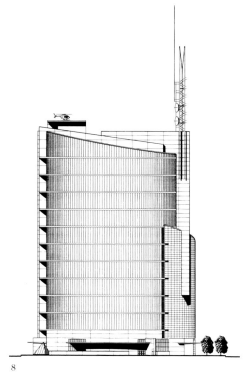

8

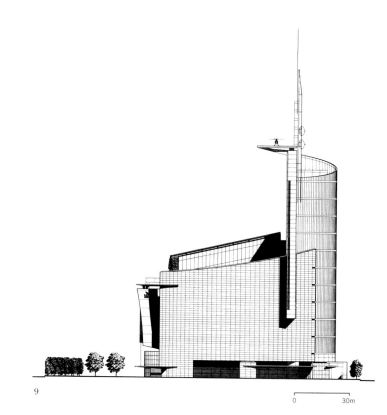

9

0   30m

10

11

12

13

IBM World Headquarters

Design/Completion 1995/1997
Armonk, New York
IBM Corporation
280,000 square feet
Stainless steel, glass, aluminum
Polished granite, fieldstone

With this building we attempted to intensify the dialogue between nature and technology. The site was adjacent to a wooded rocky ravine of weighty visual drama. The program, office space for one of the world's leading computer companies, encouraged us to express the cutting edge of technology.

Our strategy was one of "woven juxtaposition," which countered the natural landscape with the sharpness and lightness of stainless steel. However, we also faceted and fractured the surfaces of the structure to interweave with the facets and fractures of the natural site. At one level we sought contrast; on another level we attempted an interlock.

The building is composed of stretched, tendon-like horizontal elements which bind together key points of the site.

Continued

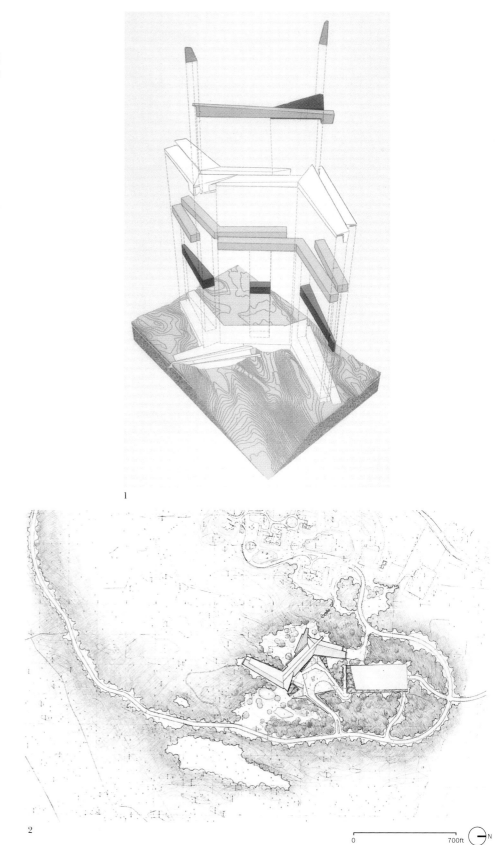

1

2

0   700ft   N

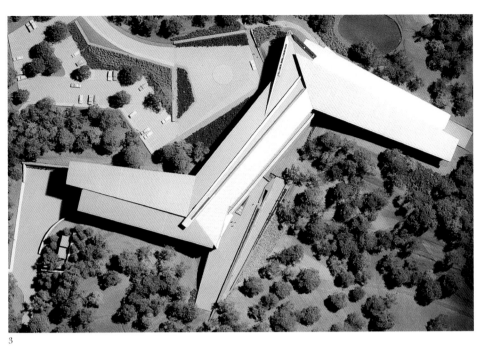

3

1 Building organization
2 Site plan
3 Model: plan view
4 Model looking south
5 Model looking northwest
6 Organizing elements, spatial definition,
  and wedge-shaped cores

4

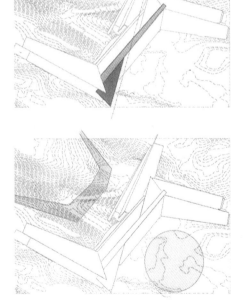

5

6

Anchored to the earth by a stone base, these tempered horizontals move across the land with the intensity of a lightning strike. They culminate in a prismatic roof surface which attempts to capture the spirit of a changing sky.

The distinction between roof and wall is erased in an effort to achieve a greater visual unity. The bond between architecture and nature is further strengthened by landscape interventions.

William Pedersen, Jerri Smith, Doug Hocking

7

8

7   Lobby ceiling and skylights
8   Lobby study model
9   Study model: skylights at lobby
10 Section at lobby and stair
11 Section at lobby skylight

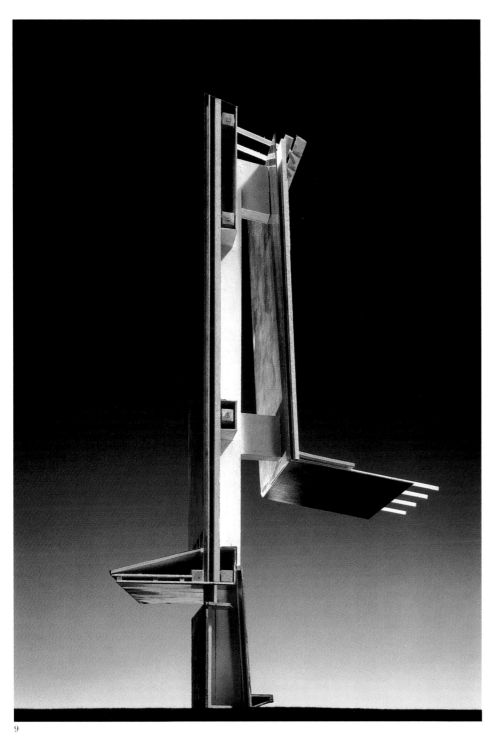

9

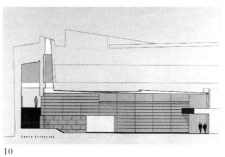

10

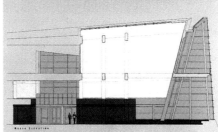

11

12

12 Third floor plan
13 Ground floor plan
14 Prow at lobby and boardroom
15 Model at entry court
16 Model at ravine
17 Dynamics of layered building and site
18 Metal roof stretches and wraps down in contrast
   to restraint at curtainwall

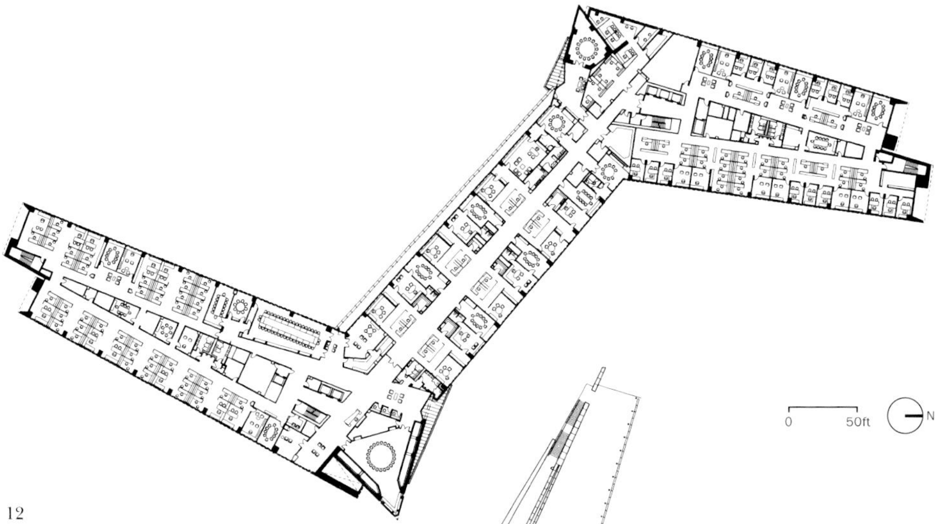

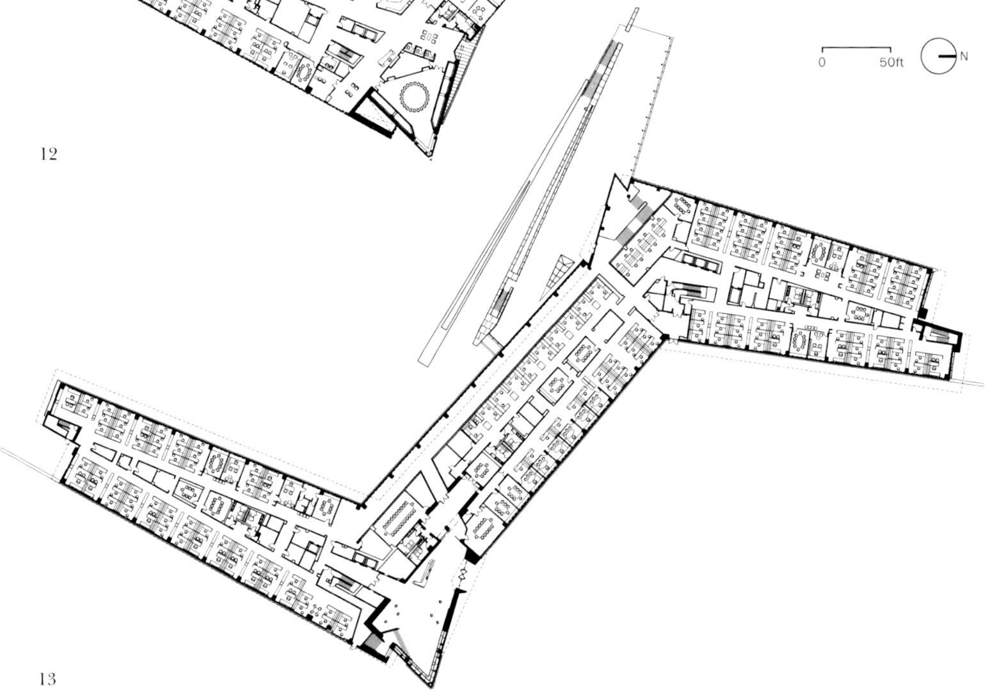

13

14

15

16

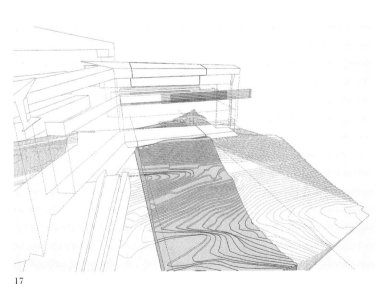

17

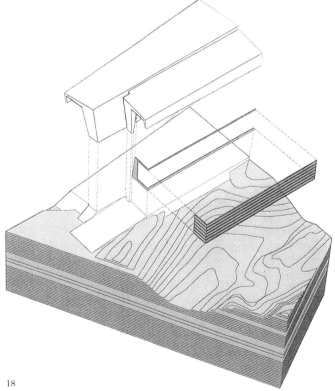

18

Baruch College New Academic Complex

Design/Completion 1995/2000
New York, New York
City University of New York
Dormitory Authority of the State of New York
712,000 square feet
Painted corrugated steel, aluminum curtainwall, reflective glazing, brick, granite, limestone
Painted gypsum board, sandblasted glass, clear glass, maple veneer, terrazzo floor

The heart of this building is a great central room which twists and steps vertically to the roof, reaching beyond to the sun. This room connects three dominant pieces of the building: the business school; the school of science, literature and arts; and the shared social amenities. This room is symbolic of the Baruch community. It is a vertical interpretation of the traditional college quadrangle.

The building occupies almost a full block between 24th and 25th Streets along Lexington Avenue. The New York City zoning code for this district established the parameters for the building's form.

Continued

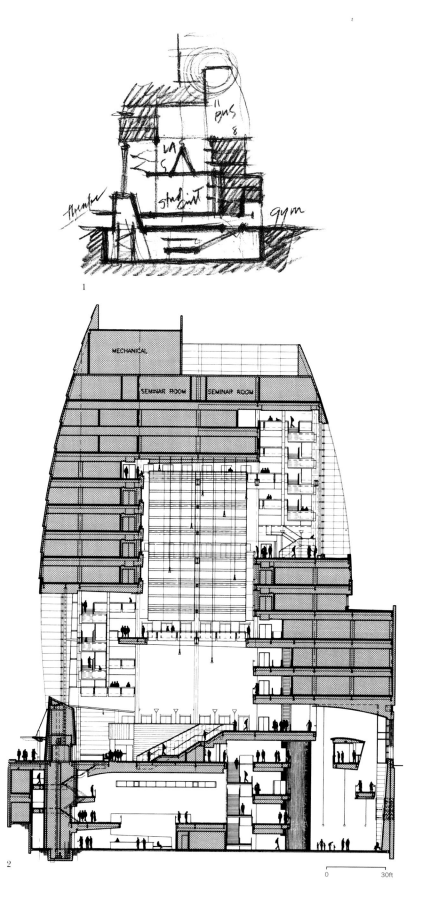

1

2

1   Conceptual sketch showing section through vertical campus
2   Building section through vertical quads
3   Eighth floor plan: business school quad
4   Fifth floor plan: liberal arts quad
5   Ground floor plan
6   Model: view down 25th Street towards Lexington Avenue
7   Model: view of 24th Street south entrance at Lexington Avenue and 24th Street
8   Model: view from corner of Lexington Avenue and 25th Street

0   30ft

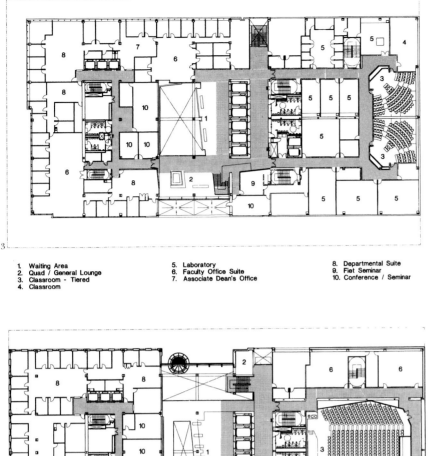

1. Waiting Area
2. Quad / General Lounge
3. Classroom - Tiered
4. Classroom
5. Laboratory
6. Faculty Office Suite
7. Associate Dean's Office
8. Departmental Suite
9. Flet Seminar
10. Conference / Seminar

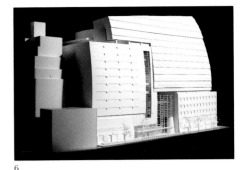

6

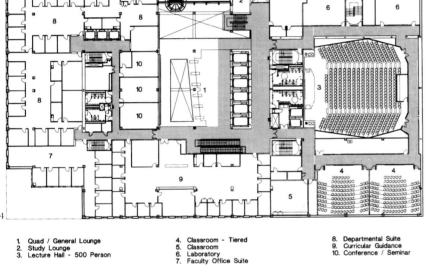

1. Quad / General Lounge
2. Study Lounge
3. Lecture Hall - 500 Person
4. Classroom - Tiered
5. Classroom
6. Laboratory
7. Faculty Office Suite
8. Departmental Suite
9. Curricular Guidance
10. Conference / Seminar

7

25th Street

Lexington Ave.

24th Street

1. Main Lobby
2. South Lobby
3. Entrance to Performing Arts Facility
4. Entrance to Physical Education Facilities
5. Physical Education Quad
6. Student Lounge
7. Bookstore / Copy Shop
8. Food Service - Seating
9. Food Service - Servery & Kitchen
10. Loading Dock
11. Multi-purpose Rm.
12. Security

0   30ft

N

8

To counter the effect of this massive form, the whole is divided into a series of parts, each identifying an important aspect of the building's use. Two monumental windows, piercing the north and south facades, reveal the position of the central room. Through these giant apertures, the school's activity can be viewed.

Externally, the building is a juxtaposition of stone and brick on the lower levels. The upper, curved portions of the structure are clad with vertically corrugated metal walls, creating a macro-scaled shingled layering.

William Pedersen, Gabrielle Blackman

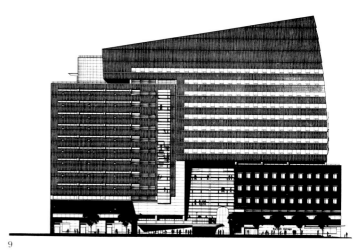

9

9   25th Street elevation
10 Stainless steel cone demarcating theater entry
11 24th Street elevation
12 Model: view of southeast corner
13 Model: view of northwest corner
14 Lexington Avenue elevation
15 Detail section through curved metal wall
16 Detail section through shingled metal wall

10

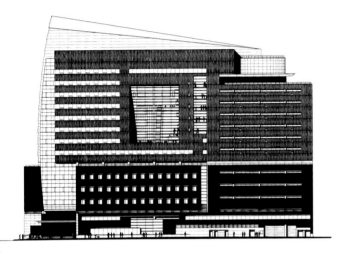

11

14

0   30ft

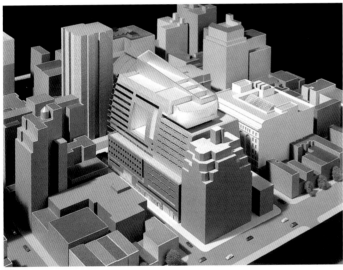

12

15

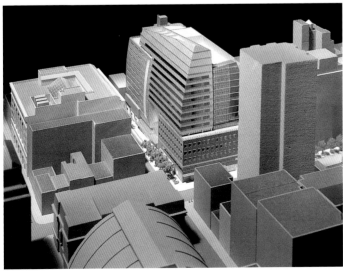

13

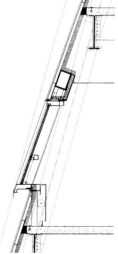

16

New Law School Building, University of Washington

Design/Completion 1996/1999
Seattle, Washington
University of Washington New Law School
196,000 square feet
Steel and load-bearing shear walls
Brick and limestone exterior wall, metal roof

The campus of the University of Washington in Seattle is dominated by Collegiate Gothic architecture, and all new buildings are required to respond to this aesthetic. Our response attempts to abstract the compositional traits of the Gothic; namely, pointed, angular, and vertically-striated forms. These characteristics are translated into both plan and elevation.

The site stands alone at the edge of the campus core. In contrast to the existing academic structures, which join with other structures to create larger quadrangle spaces, the New Law School Building must create its own external space. The geometry of this building acknowledges two dominant campus grids: the grid of the old quadrangle, and the larger urban grid which surrounds the campus.

Continued

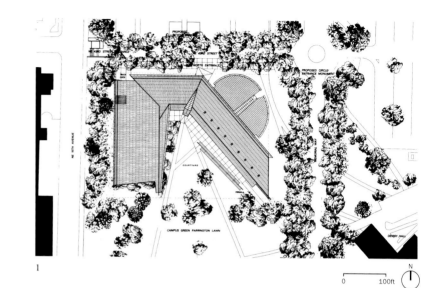

1

0   100ft   N

2

3

0   24ft

1 Site plan
2 Courtyard from Parrington Green
3 South elevation and courtyard
4 Campus figure-ground plan
5 Fifth floor plan
6 Main level composite plan
7&8 Final scheme model
9 Northeast elevation

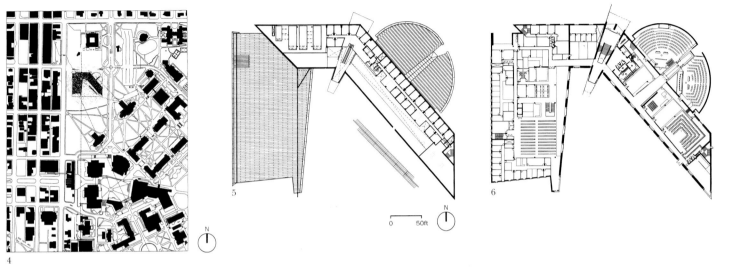

The building's two main functions, the library and the academic facilities, are gathered around a south-facing exterior space. This space is expressive of the school's community and is bounded, at ground level, by circulation galleries leading to the lecture halls and library study spaces.

Externally, vertically-organized fenestration and patterned brick relate to existing campus textures.

William Pedersen, Jerri Smith

10

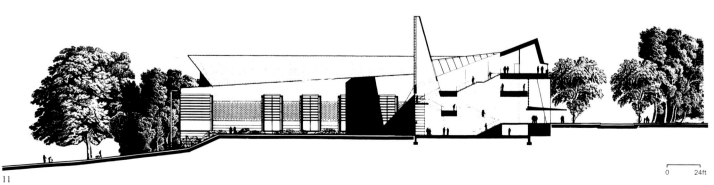

11

0   24ft

10 Library alcove and rainwater display at
   scupper
11 Section through lobby and library: east
   elevation
12 Lobby and stair tower study model
13&14 Schematic design model
15 Library west elevation

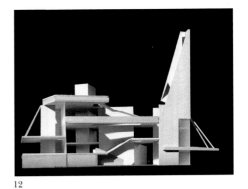

12

13

14

15   0   24ft

Daewoo Marina City 21/Suyoung Bay Landmark Tower Competition

Design/Completion 1996/2002
Pusan, Korea
Daewoo Corporation
241,540 square meters
Pewter-colored glass, painted aluminum mullions, stainless steel canopies, granite base

The great height and size of this building led to our decision to design a form of monolithic simplicity, as we had done with the World Financial Center in Shanghai. The abstract form of the building was in part derived from visual influences found in Korean culture as well as from the physical characteristics of the specific site.

Our examination of many artifacts of Korean culture, revealed a sensibility dedicated to expressing the dialogue between man and nature as an elegantly curving line. Pottery, sculpture, painting, costume, and architecture are linked by this formal motif. We strove to continue this tradition.

Located on the southern tip of the Korean peninsula, on land adjacent to the yachting course of the 1988 Olympic Games, the site faces south to the sea and north to the mountains. The north–south axis of the site is further strengthened by its alignment with a major transportation causeway crossing the bay.

Continued

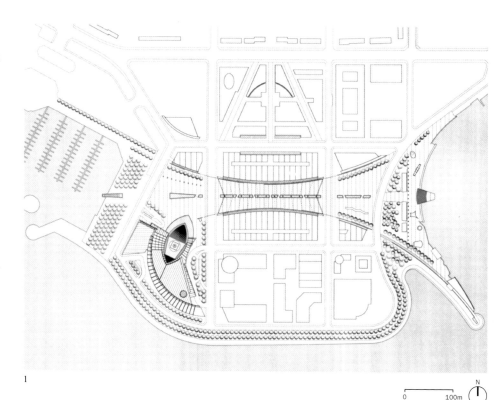

1

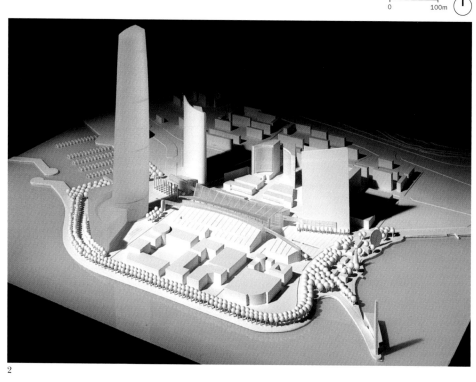

2

1   Master plan
2   Oblique view of master plan from southeast
Opposite:
    View of tower from plaza (northeast)

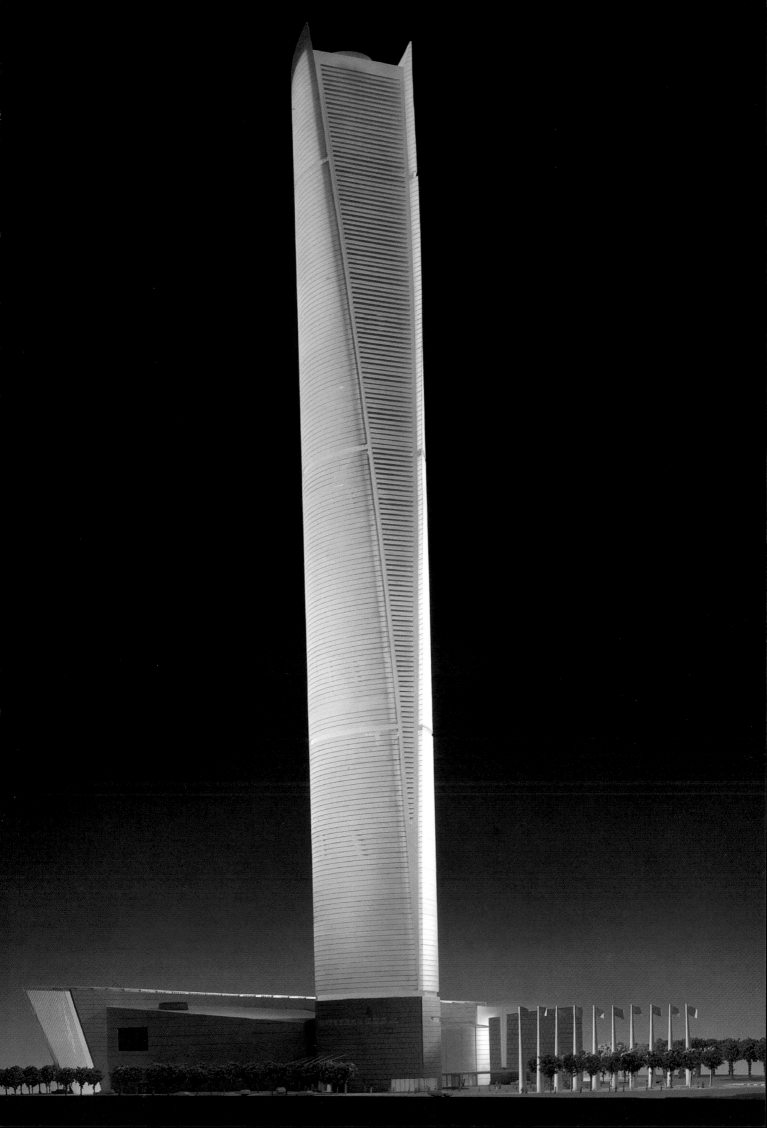

The building's form was created primarily by the intersection of an extended iris-shaped shaft with asymmetrically curving planes. The resulting tower is shaped in the form of a giant wing or sail. The dominant longitudinal axis of this form implies a connection between the sea and the mountains. Functionally, the building's larger lower levels provide flexible office space, while the smaller upper floors, hollowed by a north-facing atrium, create efficient hotel use.

This form is further augmented by the addition of a heavy stone base which drops into a surrounding pool (symbolic of Korea's position as a peninsula). The tower is terminated by a large glass-enclosed void (for gallery and observation functions). Clustered at the tower's base are surrounding structures housing a concert hall, retail space, and a major museum.

William Pedersen, Robert Whitlock, Tomas Alvarez

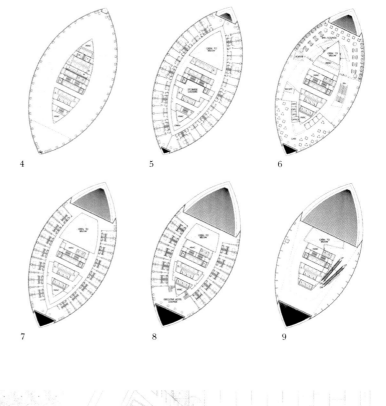

4   5   6

7   8   9

10

11

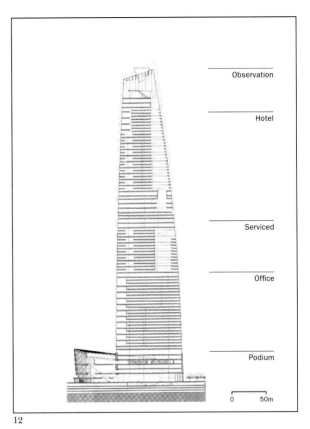

12

13

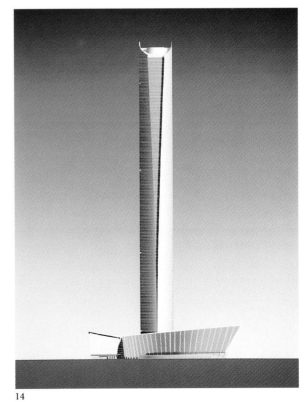

14

Rodin Pavilion at Samsung Headquarters Area Renovation

Design/Completion 1995/1997
Seoul, Korea
Samsung Group
1,115 square meters
Glass, stainless steel

The design of this small glass pavilion evolved from the placement of two famous pieces of sculpture by Auguste Rodin. The tension created between the frontality of *The Gates of Hell* and the spatiality of *The Burghers of Calais* suggested an architecture of gesture and dance. We interpreted this juxtaposition as a kind of *pas de deux* between two glass walls. Though similar in execution, the walls respond to different conditions of movement and enclosure. To heighten the experience of the museum as a place of contemplation and spirituality, we cast the space in a diffuse light by constructing the walls and ceiling in glass with varying degrees of translucency. The all-glass roof, supported by steel columns, is conceived as an independent element in contrast to the organic forms of the walls. The space created by this confluence of material and form is characterized by the contrast between the serenity of the diffuse light and the fluidity of the dynamic walls.

Continued

1

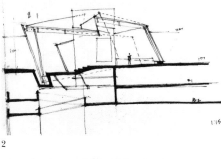

2

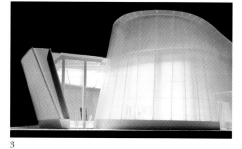

3

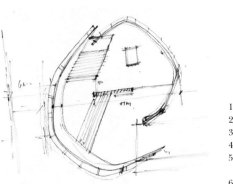

4

1 Model view from northeast
2 Conceptual sketch of section
3 Museum entrance
4 Concept sketch of plan
5 Northeast view showing connection to shopping concourse
6 Interior rendering showing *The Burghers of Calais*

5

6

Rodin Pavilion at Samsung Headquarters Area Renovation   103

The Samsung Center is composed
of three buildings situated in the middle
of downtown Seoul: the Samsung Life
Insurance Building, the Samsung
Headquarters, and the Joong-An Industry
Building. The Rodin Pavilion is part of
a larger assemblage of glass interventions
designed for the new center. Our design
creates an urban place through the form,
material, and location of these
interventions along the base of the three
buildings.

Kevin Kennon, William Pedersen

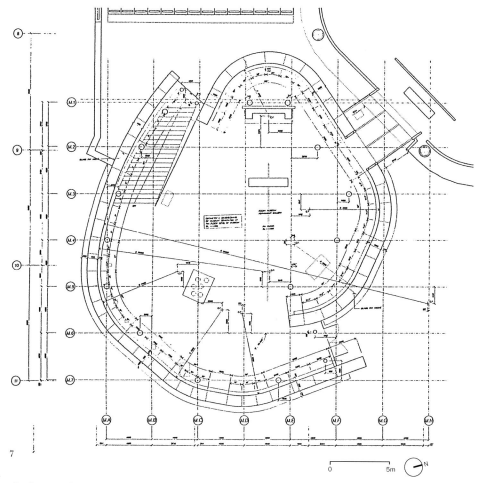

7

8

9

7 Geometry layout
8 Pre-schematic model of pavilion
9 Pre-schematic model of colonnade leading
    to museum
10 Computer rendering of interior showing
    The Burghers of Calais
11 Computer rendering of interior showing
    The Burghers of Calais and *The Gates of Hell*

10

11

12

13

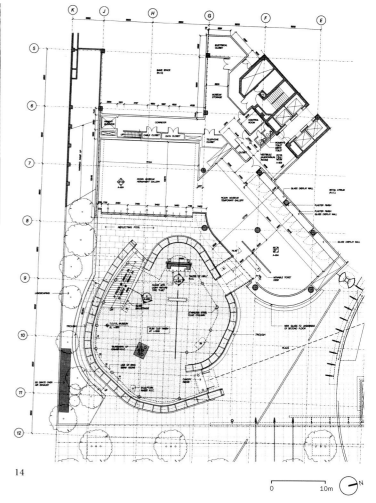

14

12 View of plaza and museum
13 Aerial night view of plaza and museum
14 Plan of pavilion and temporary galleries
15 Existing Samsung buildings along Taepyung-Ro with interventions
16 Site plan
17 Northeast view of new stainless steel entry pylons and all-glass
    curtainwall of existing Samsung Headquarters
18 Model of curved glass screen at Joong-An Industrial Plaza

0   10m N

15

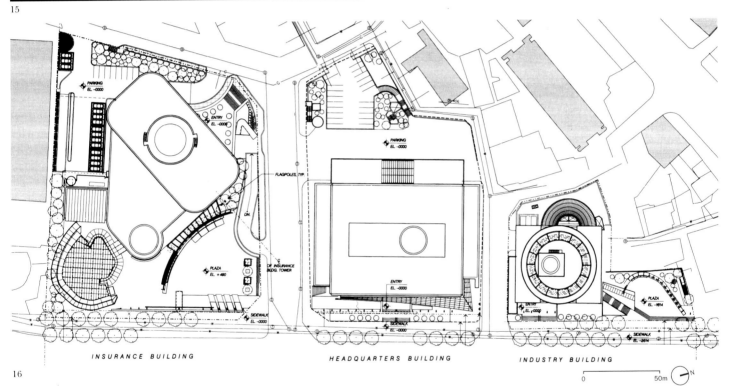

INSURANCE BUILDING   HEADQUARTERS BUILDING   INDUSTRY BUILDING

16   0   50m

17

18

Samyang Mixed-use Building

Design/Completion 1996/1999
Seoul, Korea
Samyang Foods Co. Ltd
49,700 square meters (above ground)
43,485 square meters (below ground)
Polished and flamed granite, glass with horizontally banded
aluminum spandrel

The tablet forms of Samyang were
generated according to the dimensional
requirements of a mixed-use office/
residential program and were enlisted to
organize the site according to strict open-
space and building setback criteria. The
design massing asymmetrically responds
to and includes the context around
a south garden and entry court,
emphasizing an east–west, front–back
striation of the site. The resulting assembly
creates a series of interior and exterior
thresholds as one moves from public
to private.

This layered organization became
a vehicle for referencing and exploring
the screen-like quality of spatial definition
fundamental to traditional Asian
architecture. Throughout the design
process we employed an architectural
language which only suggested the limits
of enclosure. The layering density and
scale of the various screens interact
to create intentionally ambiguous spatial
readings, obscuring the limits of public
areas and the boundaries between interior
and exterior.

Peter Schubert, William Pedersen

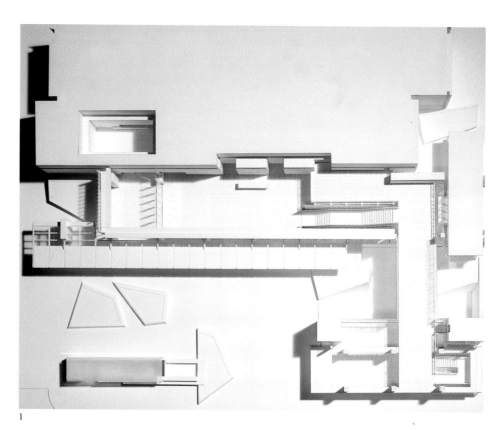

1

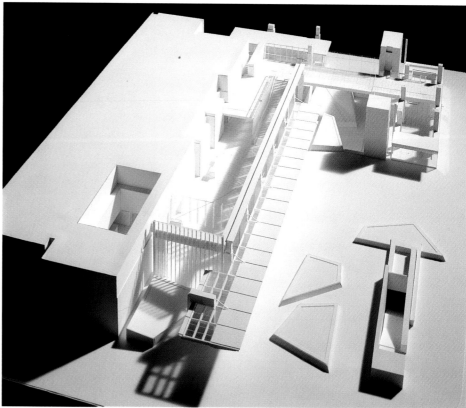

2

1 Plan view of lobby model
2 Aerial view of lobby model
3 View of tower in surrounding context
4 Detail view of tea house
5 Building section
6 Interior lobby perspective

3

4

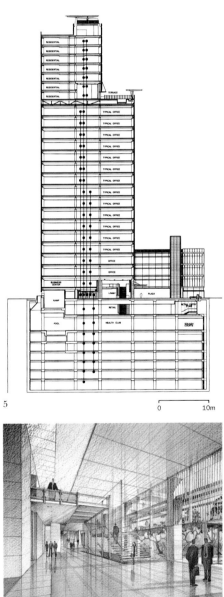

5

6

7

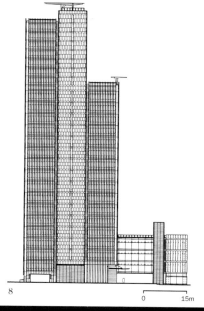

8

0   15m

9

10

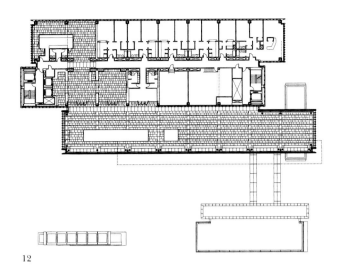

12

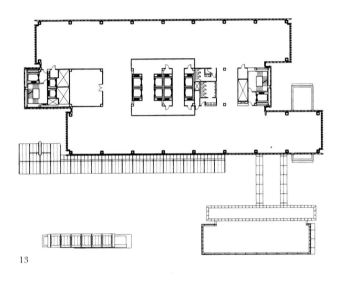

13

11

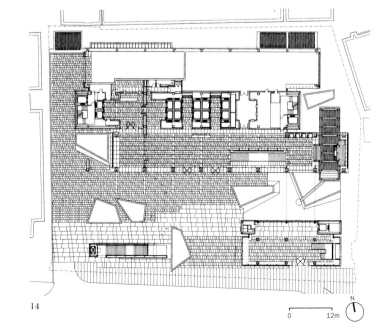

14

0   12m

N

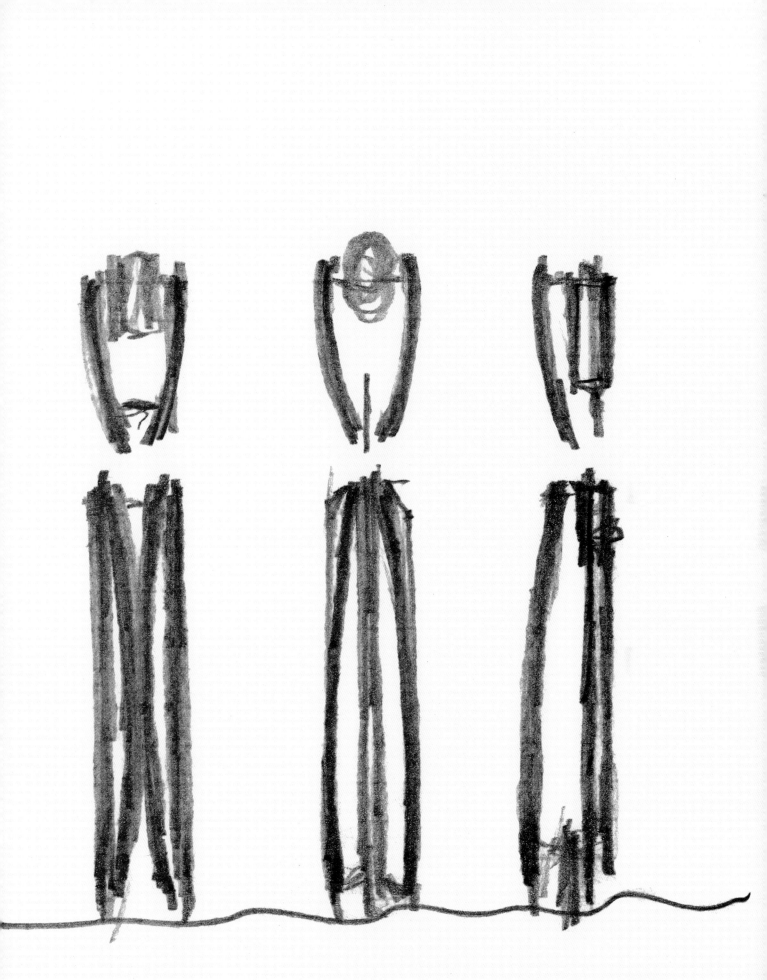

General Re Corporate Headquarters

Design/Completion 1983/1986
Stamford, Connecticut
General Reinsurance Corporation
570,000 square feet
Steel frame superstructure, cast-in-place and precast substructure
Granite podium, two-color "kynar" aluminum curtainwall with tinted
reflective IGU

The structure of this organization provided the conceptual basis for the design of its headquarters: the segmented linear bars house the multiple entities that comprise General Re, and the octagonal pavilion houses the corporate executive group. The components are arranged in a crescent shape and are anchored at one end by a circular dining pavilion and at the other by an octagonal corporate pavilion. The composition recognizes the natural landscaped hillock and merges it into the man-made garden.

The garden is both private and public and serves to mediate the scale shift across the site, from low-rise residential in the north to mid-rise commercial in the south. The broad curve of the adjacent interstate highway is reflected in the compositional sweep of the building forms. The "cupping" gesture is meant to embrace as well as lead the visitor toward the front door. The engagement of driver and pedestrian alike acknowledges Stamford, Connecticut as an important commuting business center.

William C. Louie, Ming Wu

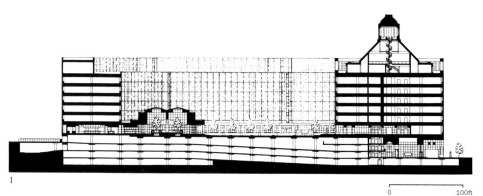

1

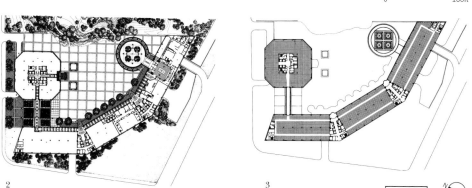

2

3

4

5

6

7

8

Mellon Bank Center

Design/Completion 1984/1990
Philadelphia, Pennsylvania
Richard I. Rubin & Company Inc.
Equitable Life Assurance Society of the United States
1,200,000 square feet
Steel frame
Granite, marble, aluminum, glass

This project started with Philadelphia's Mayor Goode, who recognized that his city was losing the race with other cities in attracting prime tenants. The 491-foot height limitation set by the William Penn statue atop City Hall had stunted the city's skyline. Philadelphia wanted a modern icon.

The site is located within a Corbusian grid of flat rectangular blocks built in the 1950s. However, it is uniquely located on axis with the old City Hall and midway between two of the four squares that define Penn Center, the context of our site. The spatial linkages to these distant cardinal landmarks recognize the order of the city. The 53-story aluminum and glass tower is supported on a five-story stone podium that anchors the tower solidly to the city grid.

The tapered tower borrows its shape from the obelisk, a monument historically used to celebrate special moments in time. A classical composition of base, middle, and top reinforces the classic iconography of the building, which dominates the center of the city.

William C. Louie, Peter Schubert, Jerri Smith

1

1   Skyward view from Market Street
2   Market Street lobby
3   Elevator lobby
4   View of top
5   Site plan showing relationship with City Hall

2

3

4

5

0   500ft   N

Chifley Tower

Design/Completion 1987/1992
Sydney, Australia
Kumagai (NSW)
116,280 square meters
Steel frame
Granite, marble, aluminum, glass, stainless steel

This project is a compositional exercise in the assemblage of parts, each part drawing its meaning from a particular aspect of its surrounding context. The timing of this commission coincided with Australia's winning of the America's Cup.

The dominant feature is the glass sail facing Sydney Harbour. Besides the implied symbolism of Australia's victory, it embodies the spirit of the city of Sydney. The wedge-shaped site on which this building sits was formed by the collision of old and new city grids. The resulting complex geometry needed resolution. Similarly, the pedestrian scale and the incomplete geometry of Chifley Square to the south needed attention. The site is also an edge site, highly visible from the harbor and the stretch of the Botanical Gardens and the Domain park to the east.

At its base, the building is composed of parts that define the streetwall; as it rises it shifts in scale and wall articulation, finally orienting itself to the larger city grid at the top. The exterior material also

Continued

1

changes from the primary expression of stone to the glass sail on the east, recognizing the building's edge position in the city context. Pedestrian movement around the base is allowed to find a natural series of paths through the arcades and galleries introduced at street level, leading to the completed civic space at Chifley Square.

William C. Louie, Christopher Keeny, Jolanda Cole

1   View from Botanical Gardens
2&3 Lobby view
4   View from Chifley Square
5   View from Botanical Gardens

4

2

3

5

Foley Square Courthouse

Design/Completion 1991/1994
New York, New York
B.P.T. Properties Foley Square
750,000 square feet
Steel frame, concrete mat foundation
Granite, marble, aluminum, glass, terrazzo, stainless steel, wood

The highly sensitive site is sandwiched between the residential communities of Chinatown and Little Italy and the Foley Square civic precinct.

The solution's basic geometry is dictated by its internal biology. The four clustered courtrooms prescribed a particular shape and required access to three separate systems of circulation. The T-shaped site allowed two basic massings to emerge: the 27-story tower housing the courtrooms and chambers faces the Foley Square precinct, while the 9-story wing housing the support agencies faces the residential community.

In the company of buildings by Cass Gilbert, Guy Lowell, and McKim Mead and White, this project borrows their color palette and the spirit of their details. In spite of its large size, a very intimate, pedestrian-scale public plaza was created adjacent to the 1903 Guy Lowell Courthouse. Since its completion in 1995, the plaza has been recognized as one of the most successful new urban spaces in New York City and incorporates the Maya Lin sculpture "Sounding Stones."

William C. Louie, James von Klemperer

1

120

1 View from Foley Square
2 Lobby hall at jury assembly room
3 Site plan
4 View from Columbus Park
5 Detail view of Worth Street entrance

4

2

3

0   100ft

Ceres Master Plan for New Town

Design/Completion 1993/2000
Beijing, China
San Ju
7 million square feet
Concrete, locally available stone, metal panel, stucco

Commissioned by San Ju, a Chinese
pharmaceutical conglomerate, Ceres is a
plan for a new town whose purpose is the
advancement of modern agriculture. The
new town is planned to occupy a 450-acre
site located at the outskirts of Beijing. It
will comprise four areas of activity: a
commercial center, agricultural research
facilities, land-use demonstration fields,
and residential neighborhoods.

The design of the new town begins with
a patchwork of small plots of land which
establish a continuous field of textured
landscape. Over this is imposed a sweeping
curved road which serves as a spine from
which various neighborhood sectors grow.
The major circular spine suggests an
incomplete form which can be continued
to accommodate future growth. The
interplay between the geometric order
of building forms and the more random
pattern of demonstration fields
underscores the utopian aims of the client:
that the design for Ceres express an ideal
of man's relationship to the land.

William C. Louie, James von Klemperer

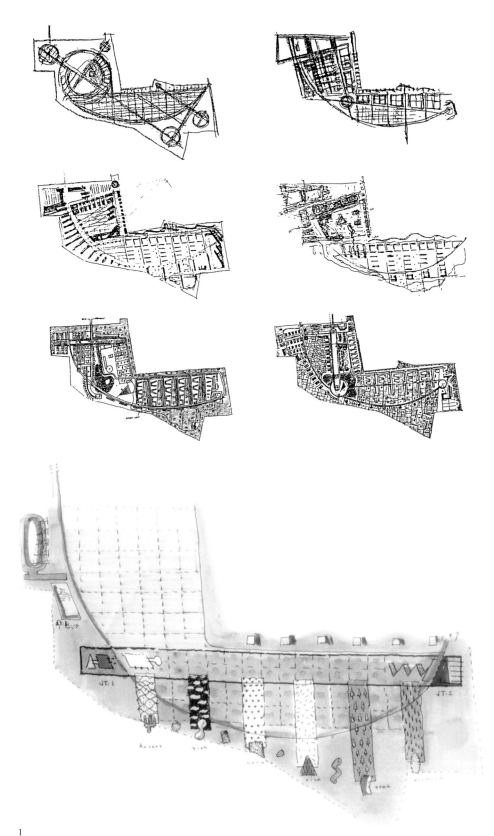

1

1 Strategic diagrams
2 1,500-meter radial diagram
3 Program diagram
4 Land-use diagram
5 Aerial model view

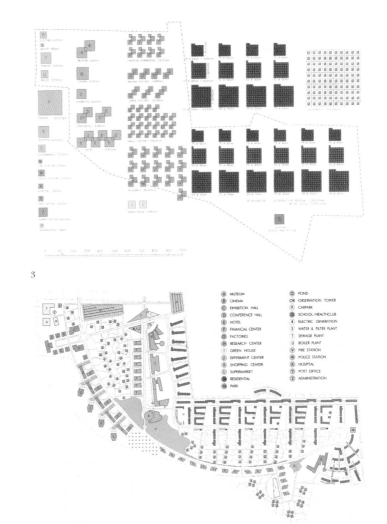

3

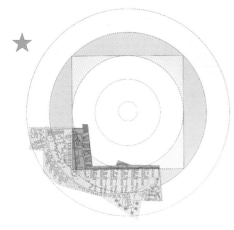

2

4

5

6

7

8

6   Bird's-eye rendering
7   Rendering view from residential unit
8   Model of central district
9   View of observation tower and commercial complex
10 View of museum
11 Aerial model view

9

10

11

Bank Niaga Headquarters

Design/Completion 1989/1993
Jakarta, Indonesia
Bank Niaga
64,000 square meters
Granite, aluminum, glass curtainwall
Marble, granite, wood panel walls

The design for one of Indonesia's most progressive banks was conceived in response to the urban and climatic conditions of its site. The building establishes its presence on the boulevard of Jalan Sudirman by dissecting its square tower mass into a series of rectilinear masses. A dominant, stone-clad slab marks the main entry, while a lighter aluminum curtainwall is oriented towards the center of the historical city.

At its base, the project is divided into a series of three-story volumes which foster pedestrian activity. The addition of a mosque creates a self-sufficient corporate compound which minimizes the need to stray into the chaos of Jakarta traffic.

The exterior walls of the building are designed to lighten the loads of the harsh tropical sun. The tower walls feature 700-millimeter-deep sun shades, while the lower masses are articulated with stone screens and aluminum shelves. As well as increasing the efficiency of the environmental systems, this brings a cool light to the public spaces and contributes to an overall experience of tranquillity.

William C. Louie, James von Klemperer

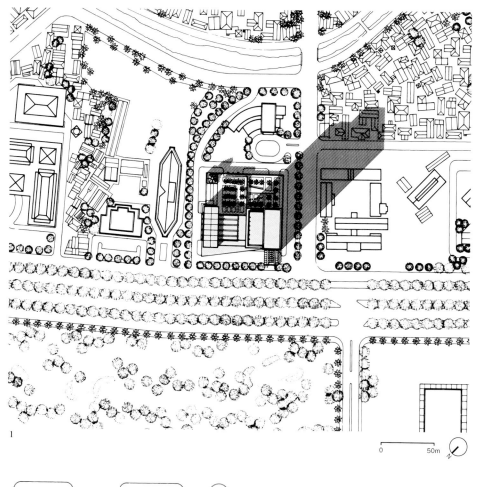

1

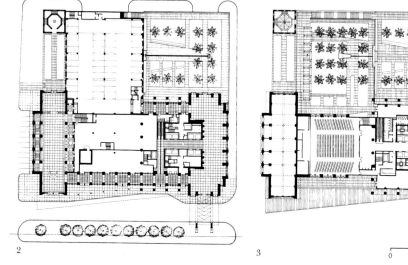

2   3

1   Site plan
2   Ground floor plan (banking hall and lobby)
3   Third floor plan (multifunction room)
4   View from Jalan Sudirman

5 Detail of *brise soleil*
6 Detail of "stitching" between metal and stone
7 Stone detail at banking hall exterior
8 Entry canopy view
9 View of mosque (background) and banking hall (foreground)

5

6

7

8

10

11

12

13

Yuksamdong

Design/Completion 1993/1997
Seoul, Korea
Dongbu Corporation
55,000 square meters
White metal and light green glass

The Yuksamdong project occupies the corner of a site at the intersection of two major avenues in Seoul's Kamnang-gu district. The design arranges four major program components—conference center, department store, office, and club—into one 22-story tower mass.

The combination of these commercial functions is expressed as a vibrant series of curved walls and volumes which spin off a central cylindrical mass. The cylinder is stabilized by its vertical surface treatment, in contrast to the horizontal striation of the accompanying wall types. The mass of the cylinder reveals itself at its base as the subsidiary masses pull apart, thus signaling the entry into the department store.

The circular forms of the tower masses are clad in a series of curtainwalls which share a common set of horizontal bands. The transformation of detail from one wall type to the next, and their relative placement, suggests a shifting circular motion and creates an overall impression of a vortex of rotating forms.

William C. Louie, James von Klemperer

1

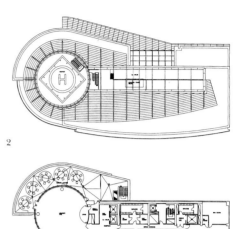

2

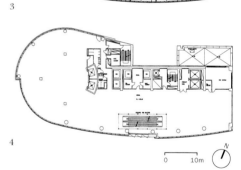

3

4

1   Northwest elevation
2   Roof plan
3   21st floor plan
4   Sixth floor plan
5   Ground floor plan
6   View from south

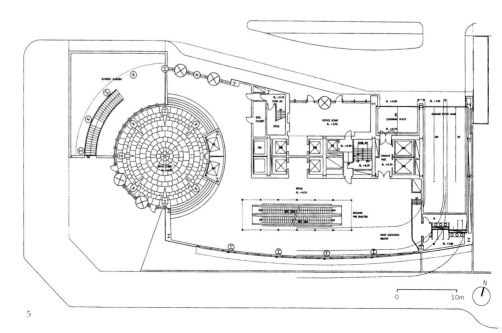

5

6

Seocho Fashion Center

Design/Completion 1995/1999
Seoul, Korea
Samsung Group
120,000 square meters
"Low E" glass curtainwall, stainless steel mullions
Calacatta Vagli marble, Korean granite, aluminum, limestone, stainless steel

This design explores the building as a symbol of its purpose. The Seocho Fashion Center is to act as a catalyst for a new fashion district that will identify Seoul as the Asian center of fashion, to rival Paris, Milan, and New York. It is the client's intent to bring the various components of the fashion world—creative, commercial, educational, and promotional—into an interactive community and to encourage a public awareness of its vision.

An interpretive attitude was adopted to express the compositional makeup of the building's anatomy. The body of the 40-story tower, clad in a neutral glass and

Continued

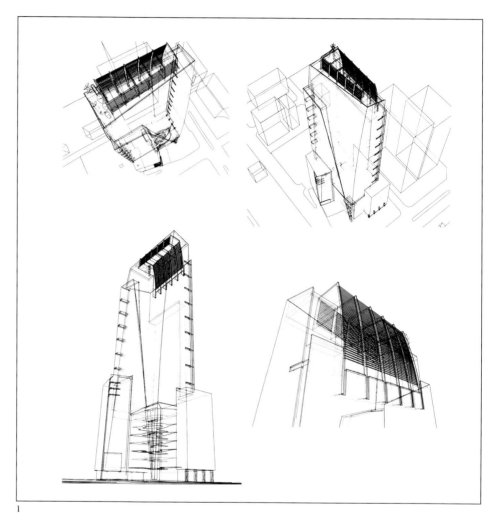

1

2

3

4

5

0   55m

6

7

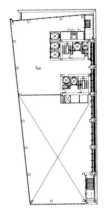

8

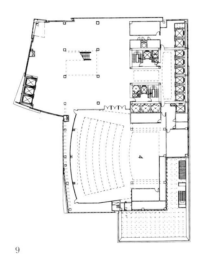

9

10

1   Computer models: massing studies
2   Conceptual phase: Option 1
3   Conceptual phase: Option 2
4   Conceptual phase: Option 3
5   Conceptual phase: Final version
6   Site influences
7   18th–25th floor plan (mid-rise office)
8   38th floor plan (executive suite)
9   11th floor plan (multipurpose room)
10 14th floor plan (sky lobby/mechanical/
    electrical rooms)
11 Ground floor plan (lobby)
12 Third floor plan (retail)

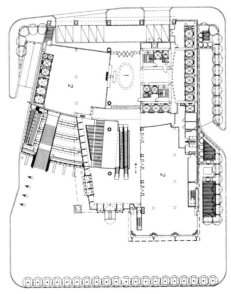

11

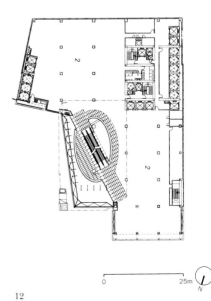

0   25m

12

metal fabric, is detailed with folded layers and stitched edges to symbolize and abstract the nature of fashion. The tower is supported by an eight-story stainless-steel-clad "leg" which marks the center of a public plaza. Products are displayed within a 10-story "retail wall" and media projections from a jumbo video screen encourage passersby to explore the center's activities. A series of escalators and express elevators bring visitors up through a multi-story atrium that gives access to retail- and fashion-related educational functions.

As a private enterprise, the project embodies the entrepreneurial spirit of Seoul and represents an enlightened association between art and commerce.

William C. Louie, Robert Goodwin

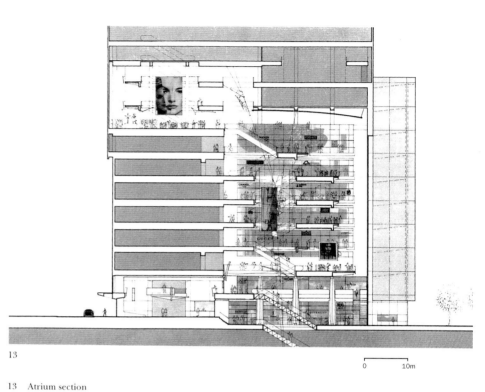

13

0   10m

13   Atrium section
14   Early study for atrium
15   Detail view of plaza and atrium entrance
16   Detail view of "retail wall," signage, and display
       area
Opposite:
       Overall view from northeast

14

15

16

18

19

20

21

Taichung Tower, Schemes I and II

Design/Completion 1996/2000
Taichung, Taiwan
Tzung Tang Development Group Co. Ltd
2,300 square meters (site)
1,150 square meters (floor plate)
Aluminum/glass curtainwall, "low E" high-performance glass,
stainless steel, vende jade marble, jet mist granite, anigre wood panels

Symbolism and hidden meaning sometimes hold greater sway than logic. The prominent site at the end of a half-mile stretch of park in Taichung, Taiwan inspired a building of poetic simplicity.

Scheme I, begun in 1992, explored a chiseled and faceted concept for a 40-story hotel and office structure. A singular crystalline form, positioned to respond to the oblique approach from Taichung Kang Road and to the park views, generated a wedge-shaped tower. The boldly chamfered top orients the tower towards the park and thus gives clues to its location in the city. This prismatic shaft is perceived to be interlocked into a granite base and anchored to the soil.

As the form of the building developed in response to site and program, the plan began to resemble the shape of a fish. After discovering that this image symbolizes good fortune in Chinese culture, we proceeded to reinforce the hidden meaning in the design and details of the building.

Continued

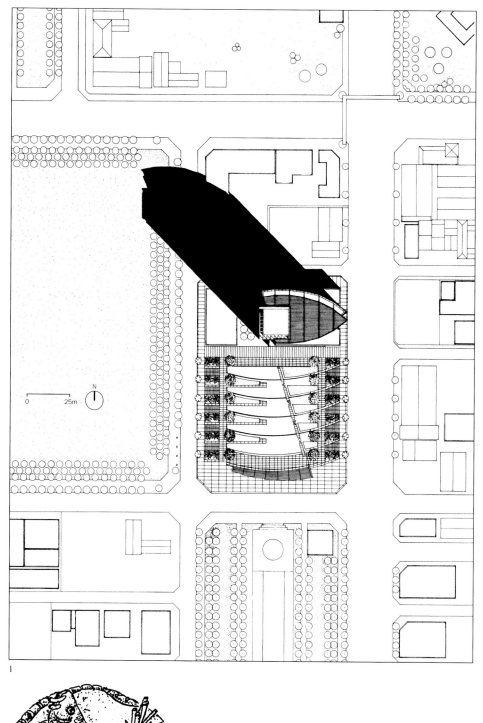

1

140

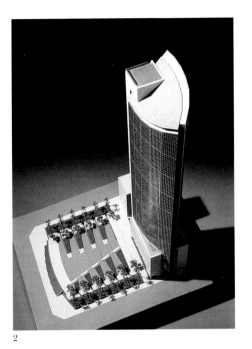

2

3

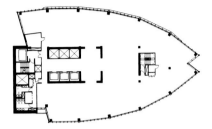

4

5

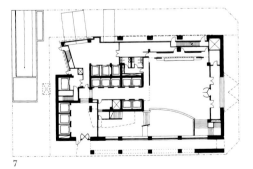

6

7

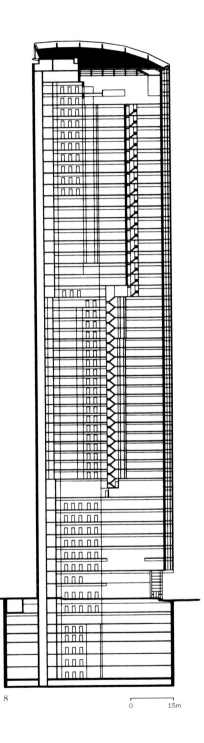

8

0   15m

Taichung Tower I

1   Site plan
2   Overall view from southeast
3   Ground level view from southeast
4   Typical office floor plan
5   Typical hotel room floor plan
6   Health club floor plan
7   Ground floor plan
8   Building section

9

10

11

12

In our Scheme II redesign in 1996, some of the internal functions were changed, but the fish shape was retained and we took the opportunity to achieve an even greater simplicity. The facets became two shell fragments fastened together, wider at the bottom to accommodate larger program functions and narrower at the top as the core reduced. This approach produced a form that curves in two directions and has a subtly elegant profile. The curtainwall is detailed as a system of rectangular glass panels; all of the dimensional variations necessary to create the spherical surface are taken up in the panel joints.

William C. Louie, Robert Goodwin

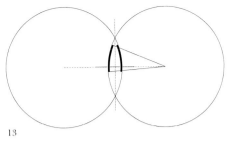

13

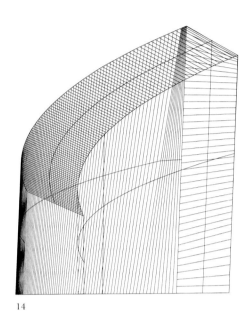

14

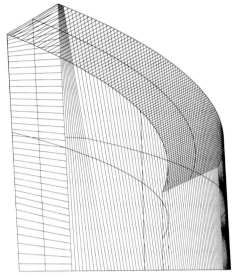

Taichung Tower II

13 Geometric study of building plan
14 Computer study of building top
15 The elegant simplicity of Sung Dynasty Kuan ware and the graceful curves in Chinese ink bamboo paintings are recalled in the form of the building
16 Geometric study of building shaft

15

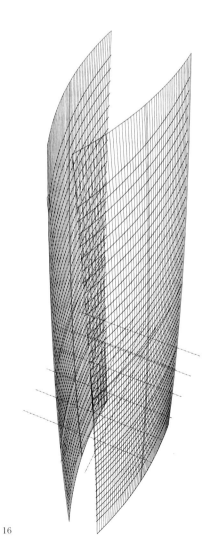

16

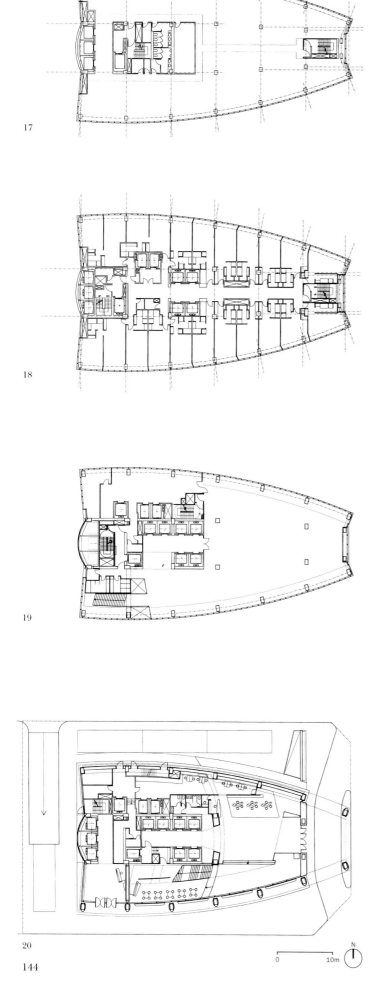

17

18

19

20

21

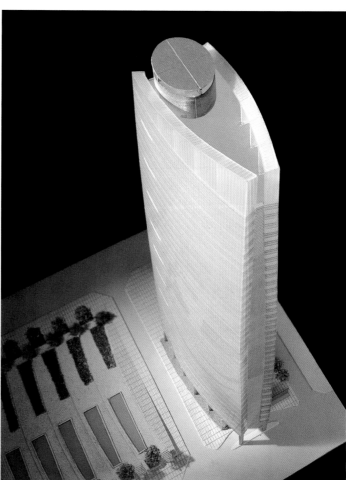

22

0   10m   N

23

17 27th floor plan (typical office)
18 11th floor plan (typical hotel)
19 Fourth floor plan (ballroom)
20 Ground floor plan
21 Model view from south
22 Model view from southeast
23 Computer model
24 Computer rendering

24

Menara Mulpha Headquarters

Design/Completion 1996/2000
Kuala Lumpur, Malaysia
Mulpha International Sdn Bhd
2,929 square meters
Stainless steel panel frame, silver/pewter-colored glass, granite, aluminum louvers
Aluminum and glass curtainwall, stainless steel panels, granite core wall

This very constricted site is located in the busy Golden Triangle of Kuala Lumpur, on Jalan Sultan Ismail, a prized boulevard of new towers and architectural incongruity.

To overcome a claustrophobic uncertainty created by the proposed neighboring buildings, a counter-form of simplicity was chosen for this 35-story office tower. This scheme's primary image is created by the two gently-curved cheek walls that converge toward Jalan Sultan Ismail. The curved surfaces bend away from the adjacent sites to relieve the tension of the crowded context. Additionally, the pinched edge is sculpted with a gently-bowed contour from top to bottom, giving it a unique profile in contrast to the vertical edges of the neighboring buildings.

Continued

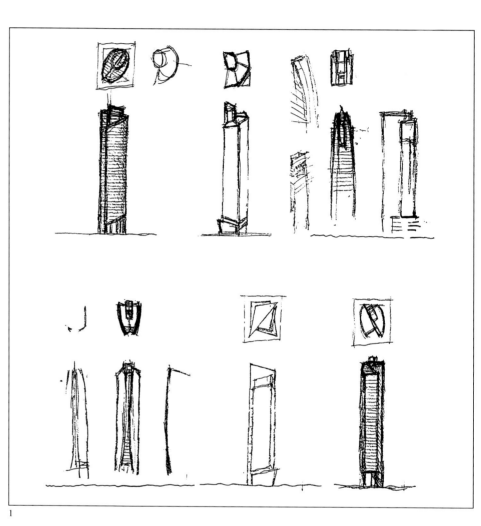

1

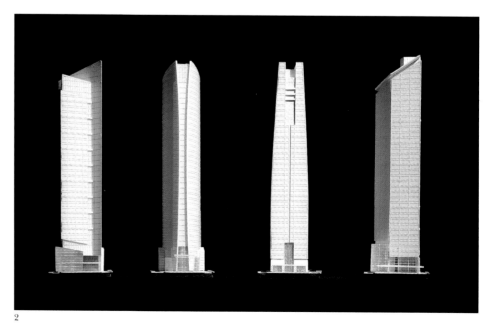

2

1 Early sketches of tower forms
2 Photographic comparisons of four concept schemes
3 Perspective view of the tower showing the proposed shape relative to its linear neighbors

At its base, through the consolidation of the tower structure into a pair of mega-columns, the main lobby is opened up and integrated into a full-site garden. High garden walls are introduced at the site's perimeter to control the views and establish a serene precinct. The strategy of simplicity, as originally explored in the Mellon Bank Center and later in Taichung Tower, here offers a counterpoint to the cacophony of shapes that are redefining cities today.

William C. Louie, Robert Whitlock

4

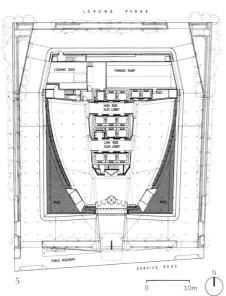

5

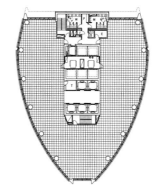

6

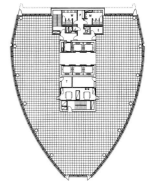

7

4   View of the massing model illustrating how
    the shape of the tower helps to alleviate the
    congestion of the adjacent buildings
5   Ground floor plan
6   Typical low-rise plan
7   Typical high-rise plan
8   Section
9   Lobby elevation looking north at back wall
10 Lobby elevation looking west at core
11 Tower viewed from the south

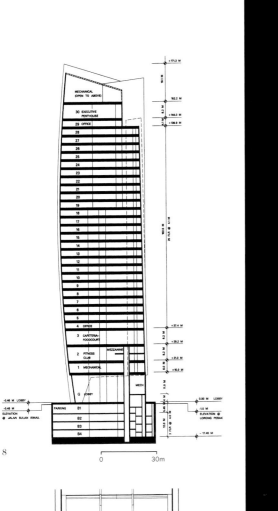

8

0   30m

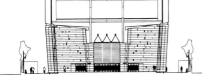

9

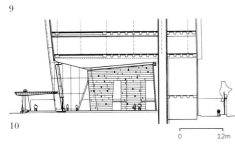

10

0   12m

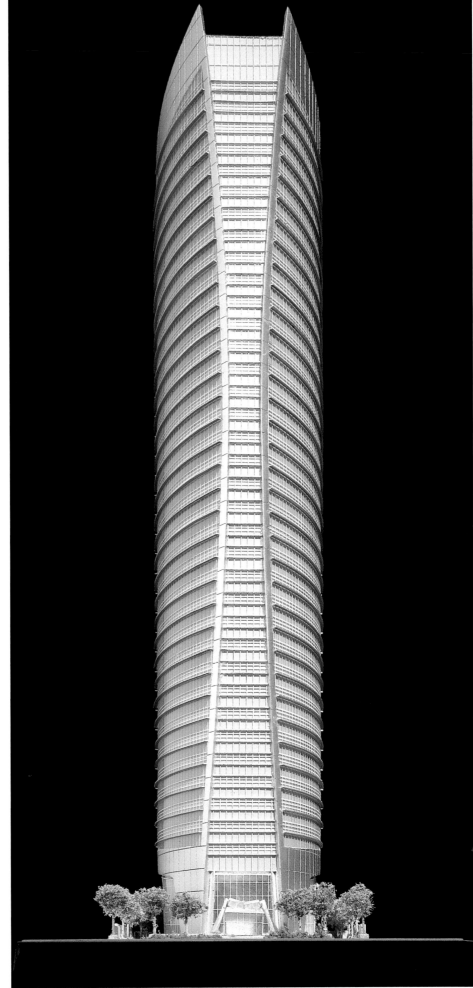

11

Hongkong Electric Company Head Office Redevelopment

Design/Completion 1996/1998
Central, Hong Kong
Hongkong Electric Company Ltd
29,000 square meters
Limestone, glass, stainless steel

The unique mid-level site overlooking Hong Kong Harbour inspires the building's double-faced composition, indicative of an earth–sky relationship. Behind the building, the mountainside pressures the solid limestone facade, folding the wall symmetrically at each end. This action, in turn, bows the taut glass face out toward the expansive sky over the city.

Within the glass facade, an asymmetrical series of elements portray activities inside the building. Three elements align to build a vertical composition. Two- and three-story conference rooms are stacked over one another, defining the body of the figure. These rooms occupy an interstitial space created by a small interior concave glass wall and the larger convex glass facade. Peeling away the reflective coating of the outer glass reveals the presence of these rooms and marks the lobby below. Engaged in an arching stainless steel roof, an observatory lantern crowns the vertical composition. A depression in the facade for an eighth-floor balcony generates the horizontal counterpoint.

Continued

1   Site plan
2   Aerial perspective rendering
3   Schematic design rendering of north facade
4   North elevation
5   Roof plan
6   Schematic design rendering of north facade at night
7   Building section

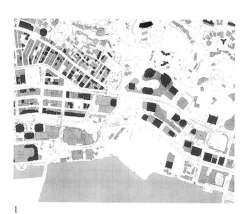

1

2

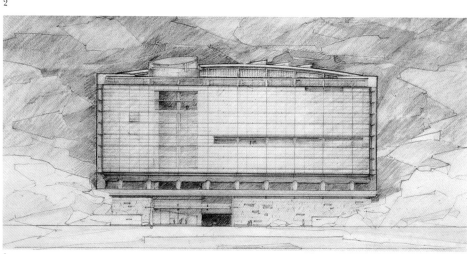

3

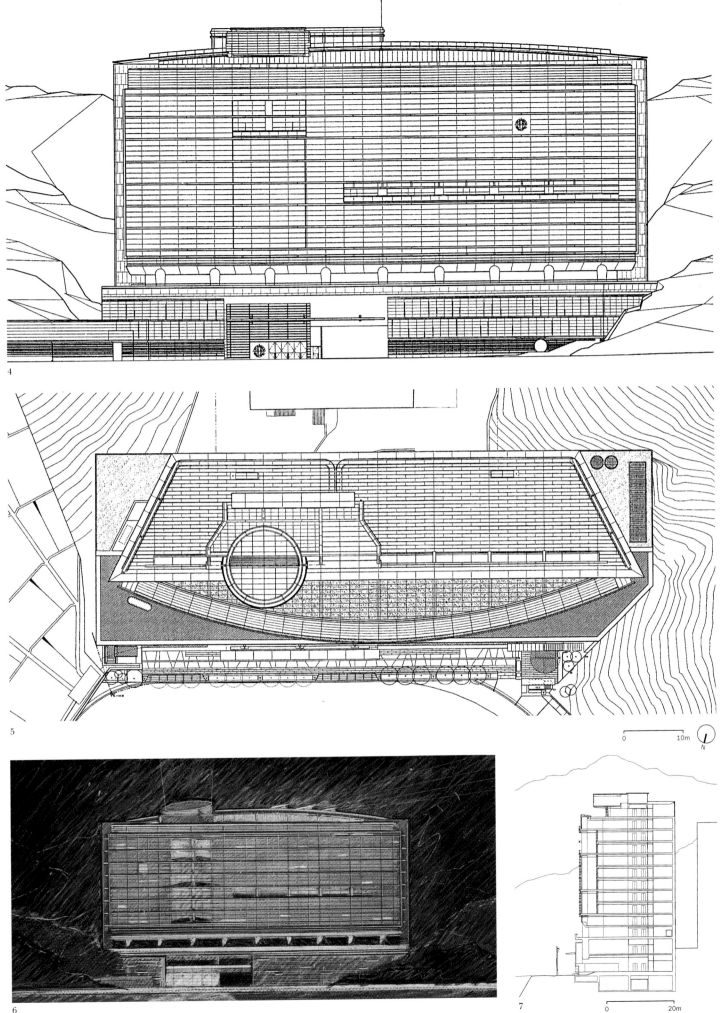

4

5

0   10m   N

6

7

0   20m

Hongkong Electric Company Head Office Redevelopment   151

Grown from the inspirational seed of traditional Chinese garden architecture, a civic plaza and garden wall draw the surrounding landscape across the front of the building and lock it to the site. The garden wall, with its integrated fountain design, provides a synthetic backdrop for a picturesque allée of trees.

While the building's base is rooted in the traditions of the past, above it grows to be a modern addition to Hong Kong's transforming landscape.

William C. Louie, Hugh Trumbull

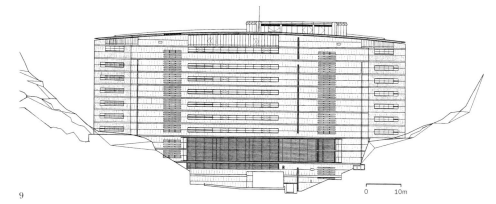

9

10

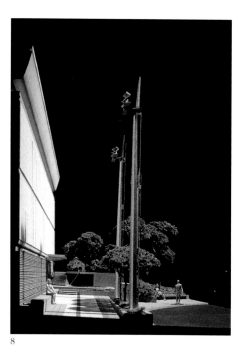

8

11

152

12

13

14

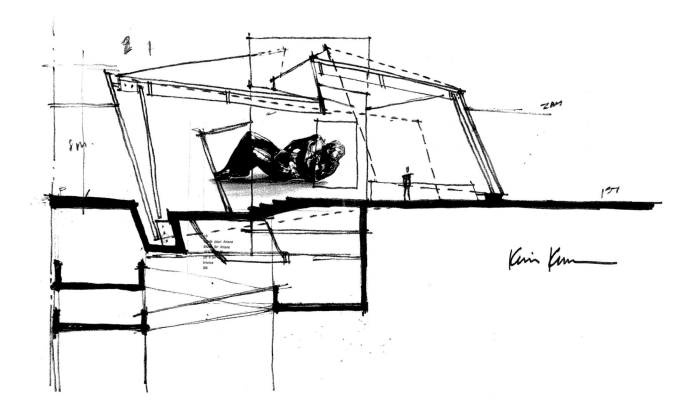

Étude pour Ariane
Étude for Ariane
bronze
3/8

Kevin Kerr

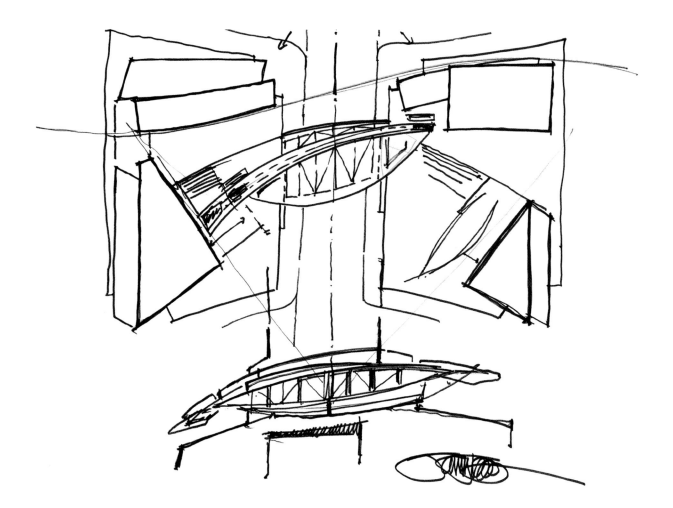

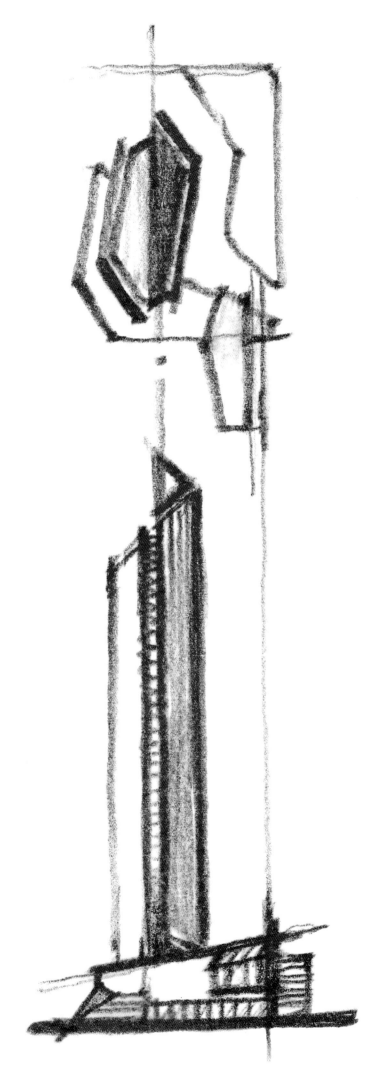

James von Klemperer

Bloomingdale's, Beverly Hills

Design/Completion 1994/on hold
Beverly Hills, California
Federated Department Stores
265,000 square feet
Silicone-glazed translucent and transparent glass panels

We were approached by Bloomingdale's to design a new type of department store. In response, we developed a prototype model which incorporates many of the design features that were later implemented in the actual buildings at Century City, Sherman Oaks, Aventura, and Beverly Hills. Our primary goals were to render the store more transparent from the street, to animate the elevation with visual display, and to address the difference between the fast pace of the automobile and the slow pace of the pedestrian.

Continued

1

1   Prototype
2   Prototype for Beverly Drive
3   Prototype
4   Beverly Drive facade
5   Beverly Drive facade at night

2

3

4

5

6

6–9 Canon Drive facade
10 Beverly Drive facade

7

8

9

10

Bloomingdale's, Sherman Oaks

Design/Completion 1995/1996
Century City, California
Federated Department Stores
231,525 square feet
Glass, perforated metal screens

Our concept was to remove the atrium space traditionally found at the center of the store and incorporate it in the elevation. This facade-atrium is a narrow space in which graphics, video, projected images, text, and goods are displayed to the public. Beyond that, our strategy was to shape the exterior using bold, dynamic geometries which express the important role the automobile plays in the existence of department stores. The use of projected images on perforated metal screens enhances the drive-by experience of the stores. Against these "fast" features, smaller-scale elements such as translucent fabric and metal canopies, curved and sloping walls, and etched glass windows are incorporated to slow the pace to pedestrian speed.

Kevin Kennon

11

12

13

14

15

11   Computer rendering: northwest corner by night
12   Computer rendering: south elevation by day
13   Southwest corner main entry
14   Northwest corner
15   South elevation

Bloomingdale's, Aventura

Design/Completion 1995/1997
Aventura, Florida
Federated Department Stores
251,000 square feet
Stucco, precast concrete panels, four-sided structural silicone-glazed
curtainwall with painted aluminum hurricane-protection screen

16

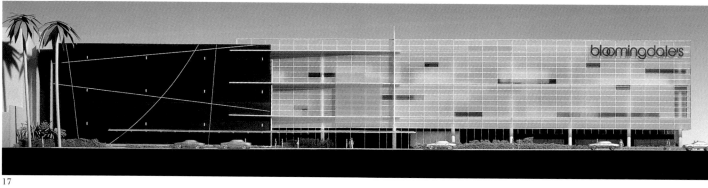

17

Bloomingdale's, Aventura

Design/Completion 1995/1997
Aventura, Florida
Federated Department Stores
251,000 square feet
Stucco, precast concrete panels, four-sided structural silicone-glazed
curtainwall with painted aluminum hurricane-protection screen

18

19

20

21

G.T. International Tower

Design/Completion 1995/1996
Makati, Metro Manila, Philippines
Philippine Securities Corporation
712,500 square feet
Painted aluminum, three types of glass, stainless steel

The G.T. International Tower was designed for a key site at the entry corner to Makati's primary commercial street, Ayala Avenue. The tower volume is composed of a series of taut glass planes which form a spiral, culminating in a dominant surface which marks the corner and forms the end of the avenue's streetwall. This plane is lifted up at the building's base to reveal a plaza at the corner, where the structural columns emerge from beneath the tower's curtainwall to frame a canted plane at the third level. Visitors to the main lobby can view the activity at street level through this plane, which is located at the top of the lobby escalators.

The dominant surface of the tower is pulled away from the building's central volume at the intersection of Ayala Avenue and De la Costa Street, creating a vertical fissure in the tower's surface which provides a glimpse of the inner volume. A 10-story vertical fin marks the tower's presence on the Makati skyline and provides a visual signature at the tower's crown.

Craig Nealy, Thomas Holzmann

1

1 South elevation
2 Rendering of third floor sky lobby
3 11th floor dining facility plan
4 Third floor main lobby plan
5 West elevation

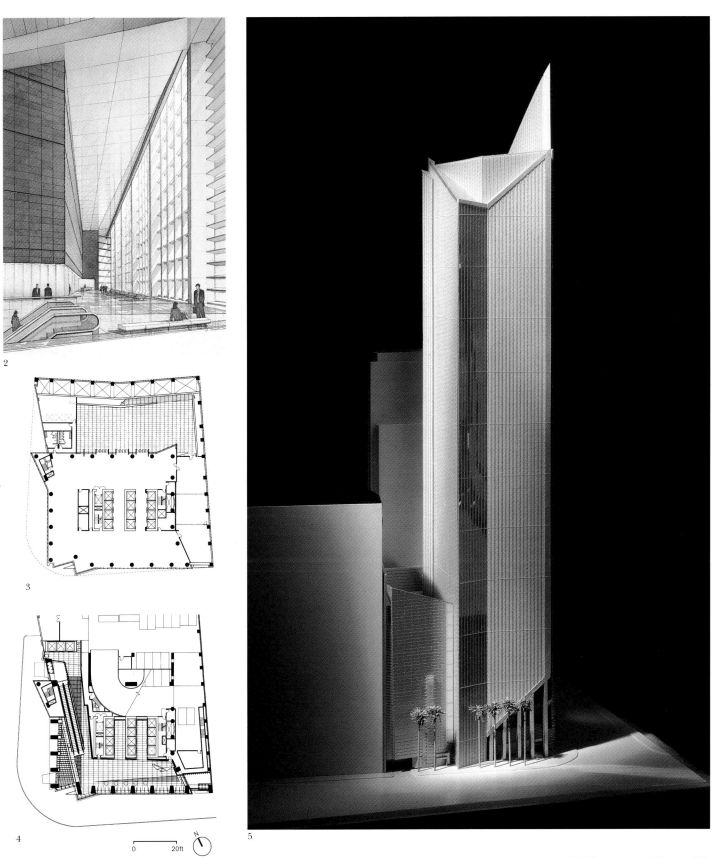

2

3

4

0   20ft   N

JR Central Towers

Design/Completion 1990/1999
Nagoya, Japan
JR Tokai
410,000 square meters
Steel, reinforced concrete
Granite, stainless steel, architectural precast concrete, ceramic tile

JR Central Towers is a project in Japan's third-largest metropolis, Nagoya. Designing the interface between a complex mixed-use program and a variety of transportation stations, including that of the national high-speed bullet train (the *Shinkansen*), is a major challenge in the organization of the project.

Located on a significant site at the entrance to the city, two soaring office and hotel towers rise from a 20-story retail podium to create an image of a "gateway." Although the two towers are different in composition and function, the strong vertical expression of the towers' exteriors and their gently curved surfaces help to unify them. Each tower has an independent urban identity, yet the two forms are in harmonious dialogue with each other.

The organization of large-scale public circulation is the key to the clarity of the project. The movement of people through the podium facade is celebrated by a 15th-floor "skystreet," which transforms the building into a "vertical city."

Continued

1

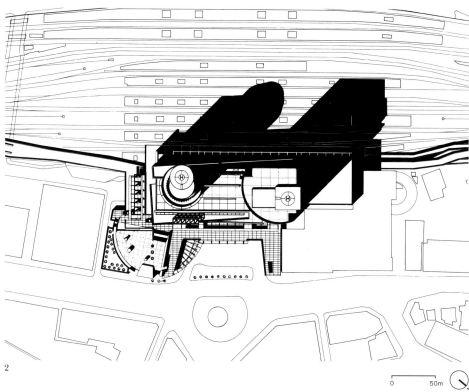

2

0   50m

3

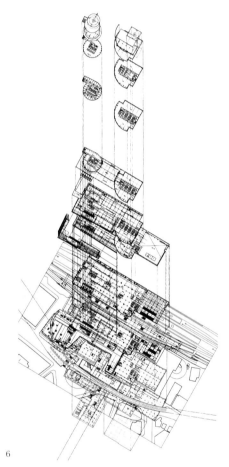

6

4

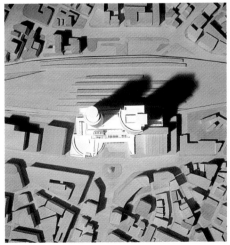

5

1   Northeast elevation
2   Site plan
3   Aerial view of model from the north
4   West view of the building model from the bullet
     train tracks
5   Aerial view of the context model
6   Extruded plan diagram

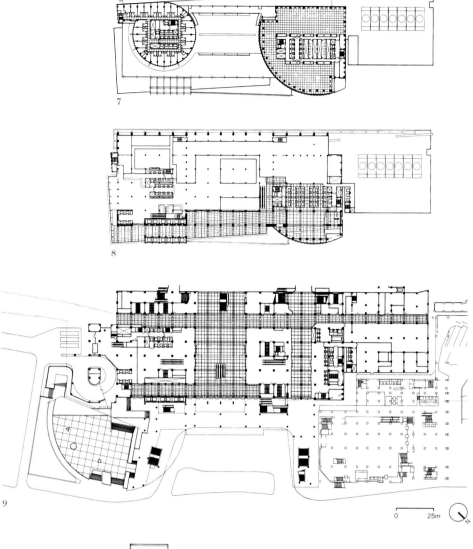

7

8

The contrast between the vertical
expression of the towers and the
horizontal expression of the podium
reflects the desire to integrate the building
into the urban context at two different
levels. Reminiscent of a long stretch of rail
lines, the horizontal articulation of the
podium provides a link to the surrounding
context. The tall vertical expression of the
towers anticipates the reach of buildings
that will inevitably rise around the tower
in the 21st century.

John Koga, Paul Katz, A.E. Kohn

9

0   25m   N

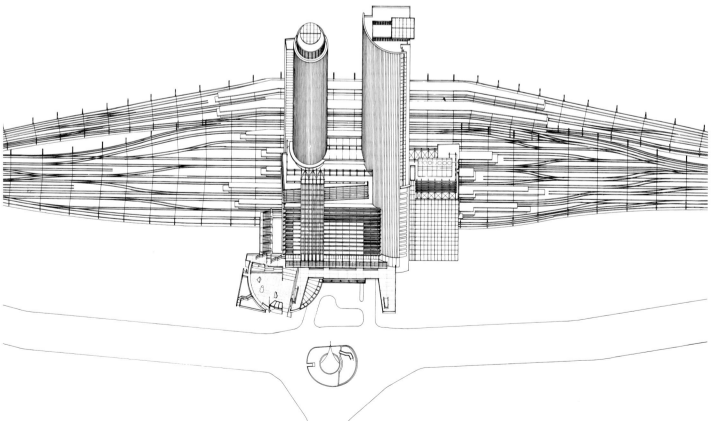

10

11

13

14

12

15

The Landmark, Hong Kong

Design/Completion 1994/1997
Central, Hong Kong
Hong Kong Land Property Company Ltd
200,000 square feet
Granite, limestone

The Landmark has established itself as one of the premier retail centers in Asia. This project involves a revitalization of the internal and external appearance of the center to respond to today's growing market and to secure its high-profile position.

At the heart of the project, a large atrium space organizes the shopping experience and forms the retail core for Hong Kong's Central district. Light, surface, and color are paramount in the design concept of the atrium. The passage of natural light into the space is enhanced by the addition of a dichroic glass ceiling sculpture, a layered array of custom louver elements, and a complete upgrade of the existing skylights.

Surfaces within the complex are neutral in color and texture to emphasize the sophisticated color palettes of the various retail tenants. Reflections of colored light, shade and shadow, and accent lighting all enliven these surfaces. Retail corridors that terminate in the atrium are refinished using the same surfacing concept, unifying the interior spaces.

Continued

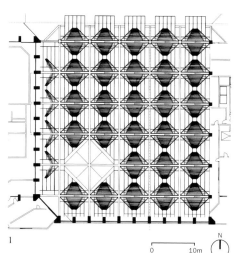

1　Skylight diagram
2　Section of atrium
3　Ground floor plan
4　Ground floor view of the first floor restaurant within the atrium space
5　Entry to retail corridor
6　Second floor office lobby arcades

0　　　10m　　N

2

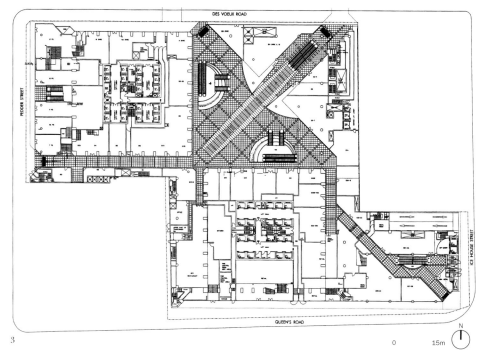

3

0　　　15m　　N

4

5

6

7 Dichroic glass ceiling sculpture
8 Ground floor storefront facade with French limestone and stainless steel
9 Central atrium

The materials used for the exterior recladding are harmonious with the interior palette and project the center's new identity into the surrounding urban context.

John Koga, Paul Katz, A.E. Kohn

7

8

Niaga Tower II

Design/Completion 1996/1999
Jakarta, Indonesia
P.T. Grahaniaga Tatautama, Niaga Tower Partnership
65,000 square meters
Concrete
Aluminum, blue-green glass, green granite

The Niaga II project, located in Jakarta, is composed of a series of parallelograms and canted surfaces. It stands in clear contrast to its Niaga I neighbor, turning away from the older arterial boulevard of Jalan Sudirman to face the newly-emerging CBD district, which becomes its front door. The 40-story tower is expressed as a glass solid which has been sheared along the north–south axis that corresponds to the two ends of the double site. This solid-core mass is then cloaked by two diagonally-opposed "jackets" consisting of deep vertical fins. These outer curtainwall jackets provide a texturally subdued backdrop which complements the intricacy of the Niaga I wall. The folded wall planes reinforce the simplicity of the prismatic forms they cloak and also reduce by 30 percent the intensity of the harsh tropical sun.

James von Klemperer, William C. Louie

1

2

3

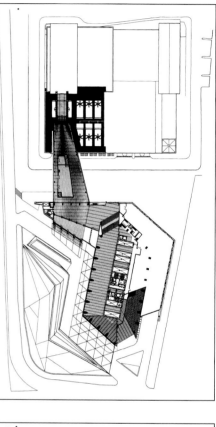
4

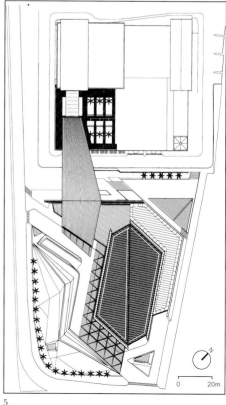
5

1   View of Mosque and Palm Court
2   East view
3   South view
4   Site plan
5   Mezzanine plan
6   Lobby perspective
7   Arrival court
8   South elevation

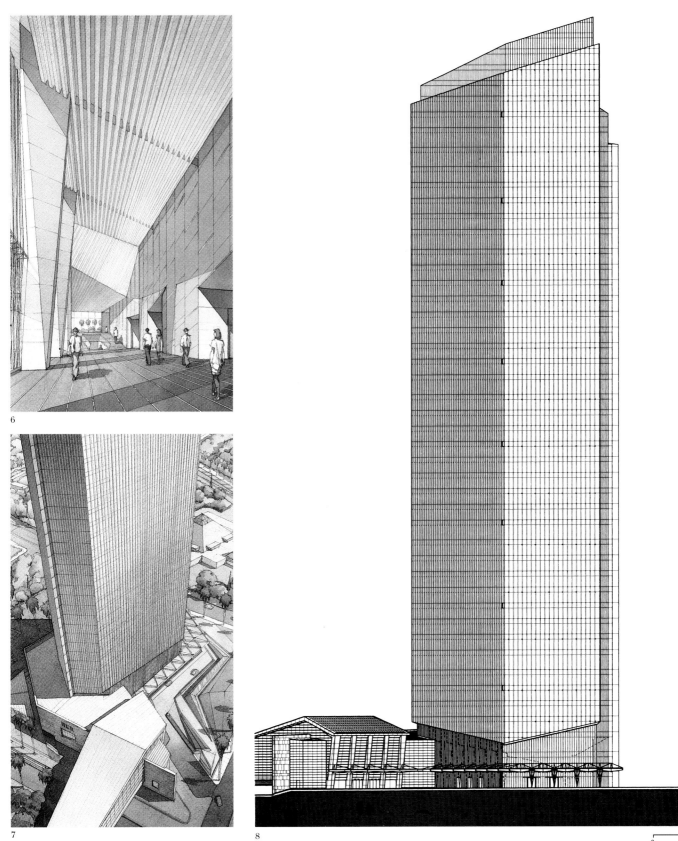

6

7

8

0   15m

Nanjing Xi Lu

Design/Completion 1994/1999
Shanghai, China
Hang Lung Development Co. Ltd
300,000 square meters
Stainless steel shopfronts, custom art glass interior shopfronts, rough-hewn Chinese granite exterior wall cladding
Terrazzo flooring, silver aluminum curtainwall, painted plaster interior finishes

The assignment of combining a 60-story and a 40-story office tower with a major retail mall in the heart of Shanghai's old city posed several major challenges, the foremost being the need to mediate between the scale of Nanjing Xi Lu, a celebrated pedestrian thoroughfare, and the scale of such large structures. The solution arranges a series of near-primary, radially derived volumes (lozenge, cone, almond, and arc) in the manner of a collage. They are bound together by a five-story podium, but each one establishes its own entry and formal independence by coming cleanly down to the ground. Each volume is distinguished by a canted sectional lean or cut. The resulting forms convey an architectural exuberance that reflects the vibrant street life of Nanjing Xi Lu.

Continued

1

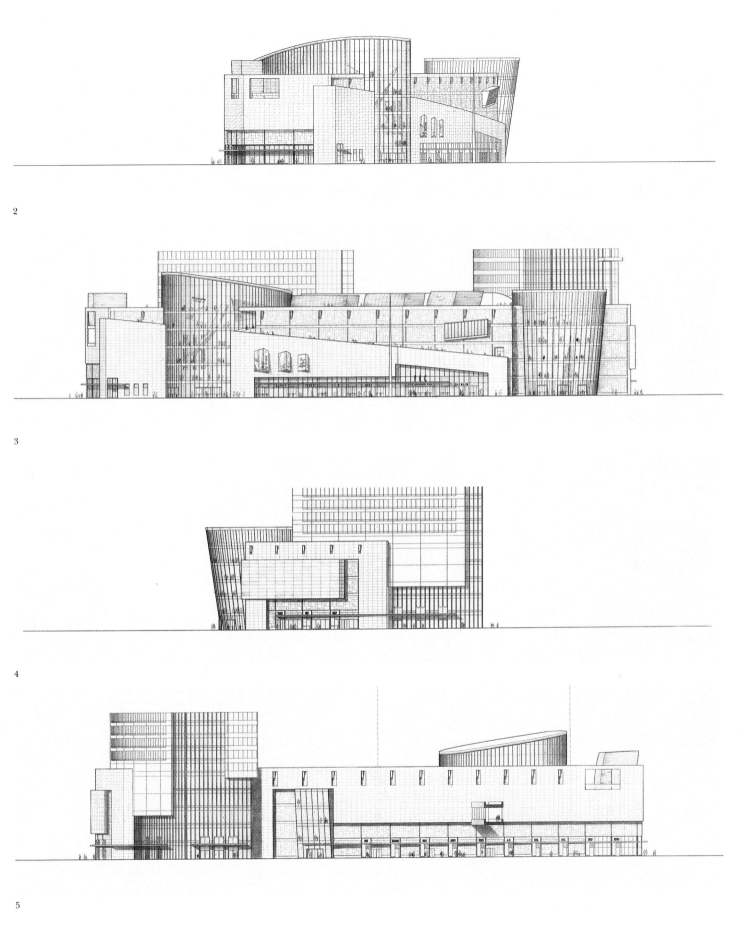

2

3

4

5

1 South view
2 West podium elevation
3 South podium elevation
4 East podium elevation
5 North podium elevation

The overall composition of the project is bound by a larger, circular geometry, as if influenced by the forces of a vortex. The resulting embrace of swirling forms gestures towards the neighboring Stalinist exhibition building and its forecourt park. The upward spiral of building masses is terminated by the translucent lantern of the taller tower. This distinct form will be seen above the city as an icon of the commercial presence of the Hong Kong client whose headquarters will be housed within the complex.

James von Klemperer, William C. Louie

6

7

6 East view
7 Location map
8 Podium: level 1 plan
9 Streetwall

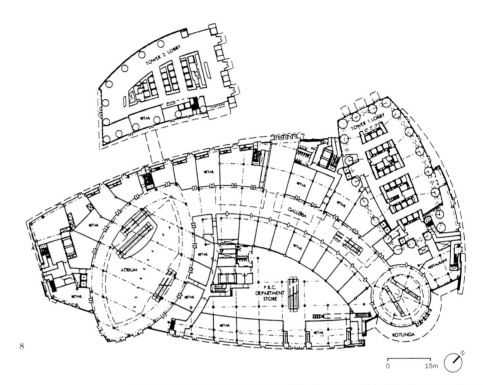

8

0   15m

9

"City Lights," KPFI, London

27 Old Bond Street

Design/Completion 1992/1994
London, England
Matsushita Investment Developments (MID) UK
5,000 square meters (gross)
2,800 square meters (retail)
1,500 square meters (office)
700 square meters (restaurant)
Exposed steel beams and concrete steel deck
Clear glass, white metal, stainless steel

At 27 Old Bond Street the two facades of a listed building were retained, the interiors were demolished, and a new retail and office complex was built. A large atrium, sloped in section to follow the right-to-light diagram, unites all floors and brings light deep into the middle of the ground floor retail area. Glass escalators rise up through this space, drawing shoppers to the upper floors.

The building is naturally ventilated: hot air rises up the atrium glass and escapes through an opening at the apex. The design of this space has been adopted as the prototype for the National Portrait Gallery. The retail component is presently the European flagship store for DKNY Fashion.

KPFI, London

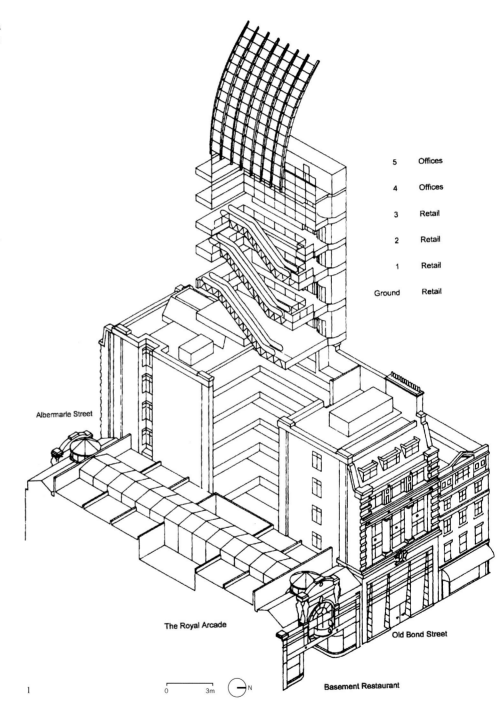

5	Offices
4	Offices
3	Retail
2	Retail
1	Retail
Ground	Retail

Albermarle Street

The Royal Arcade

Old Bond Street

Basement Restaurant

1

0   3m   N

1   Axonometric diagram
2   Atrium view

180

2

3

4

5

6

7

8

9

10

11

3   Site during construction
4   Interior atrium on third floor
5   Interior on second floor
6   Interior atrium on second floor looking south
7   Interior atrium at ground floor
8   Interior atrium looking down from third floor
9   Looking across third floor interior atrium
10   Second floor interior atrium
11   Looking across second floor interior atrium
12   Main entry on Bond Street
13   Atrium detail
14   Atrium looking across Royal Arcade

12

13

14

The Cyprus House of Representatives

Design/Completion 1994/2000
Nicosia, Cyprus
Ministry of Communication and Works
20,000 square meters
Reinforced concrete frame
Sandstone, glass, alabaster, steel

The building will be set on a hill facing the processional route between the presidential palace and the old city. The primary role of the building is to encourage citizens to participate in the democratic process. To this end, the design places the public at the heart of the new complex and brings them into direct contact with the working spaces of the institution.

Continued

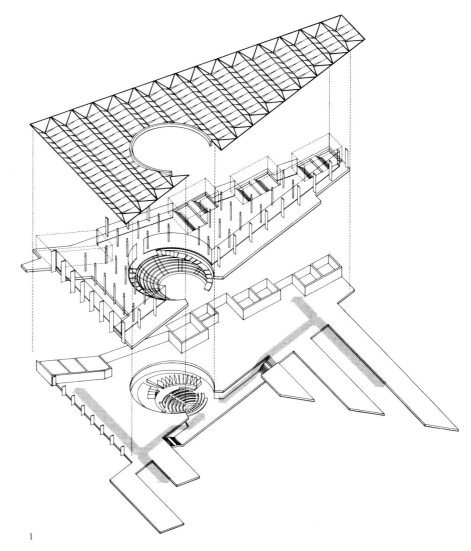

1

2

1 Extruded axonometric diagram
2 South elevation
3 Aerial view of the parliamentary garden
4 North elevation

3

4

The foyer surmounting the hill forms an extension to the public open spaces adjacent to the site. It is a space of meeting and exchange between the public and their representatives: a contemporary agora for a modern and dynamic democracy. It is flanked by the committee and political meeting rooms. At the symbolic and functional center of the building is the parliament chamber itself, a tall alabaster drum diffusing light into the hall and foyer that surround it.

KPFI, London

5

6

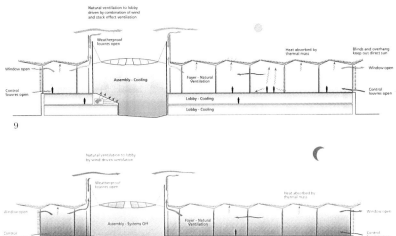

9

10

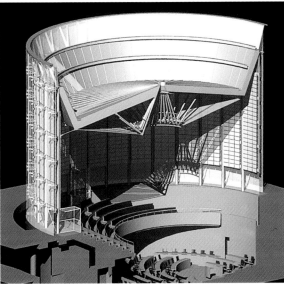

7

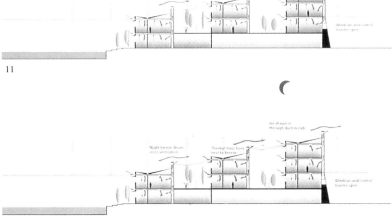

11

12

8

5 Chamber construction study: a double-walled construction is engineered to control admission of heat and light into the main chamber
6 Detail of central roof light
7 Section through plenary chamber (roof not shown)
8 Interior view of plenary chamber
9 Foyer/assembly showing environmental operation (mid-season, day)
10 Foyer/assembly showing environmental operation (mid-season, night)
11 Offices showing environmental operation (mid-season, day)
12 Offices showing environmental operation (mid-season, night)

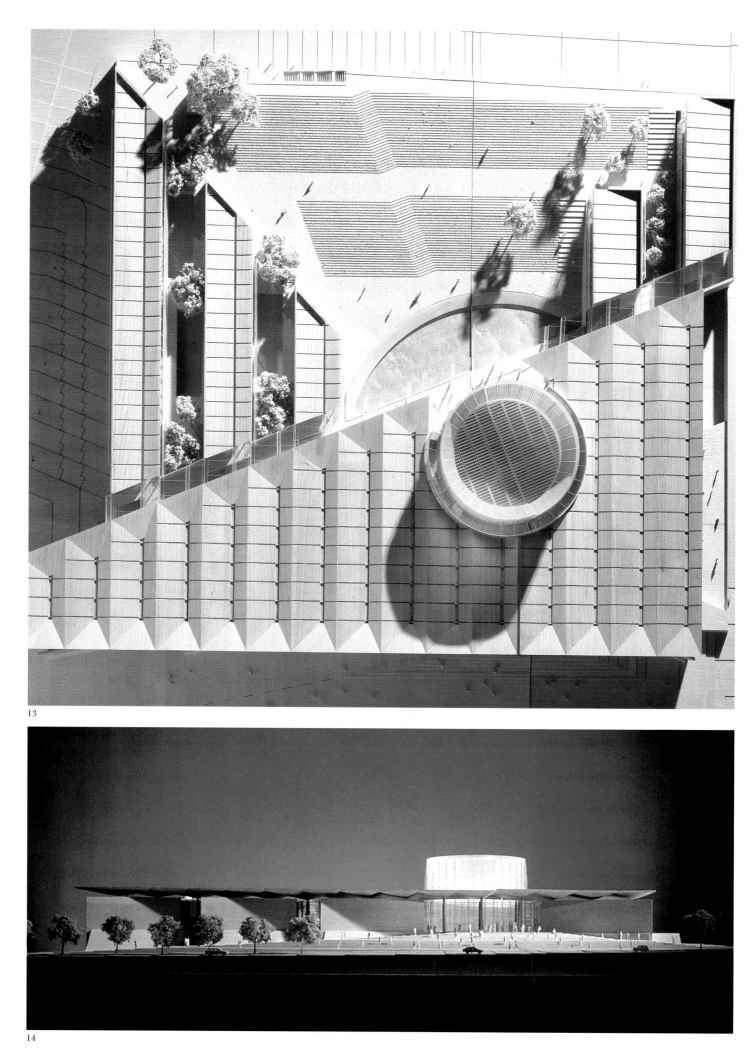

13

14

15

16

Thames Court

Design/Completion 1995/1998
London, UK
Markborough Properties Ltd/DIFA
30,000 square meters (gross floor area)
Steel
Metal, glass, stone

Thames Court occupies a prominent site along the River Thames in the City of London. Opposite the new renovation of Shakespeare's Globe Theater, the archaeologically rich site is associated with King Alfred and the early Saxons' main landing place.

The building comprises five stories above ground. A large stone portal along Upper Thames Street frames a glass wall buffer zone that protects the office space from the heavy traffic of the street. Two external stair towers break down the scale of the long side elevation. The River Thames facade continues the rhythm established along the side and steps out towards the river in a section similar to that of the entrance foyer.

The internal spaces step up from a lower northern hall to a higher southern space. The atrium roof is shaded by motorized fabric paddles. The bridges and the structure for the horizontal planes are light and filigree, allowing daylight to penetrate through the building to the entrance space.

KPFI, London

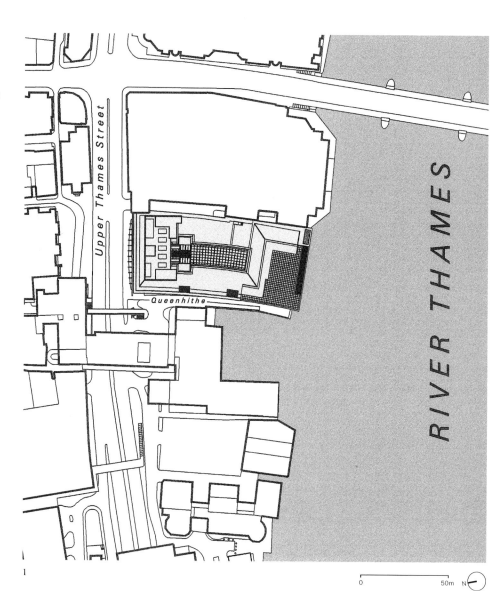

1

2

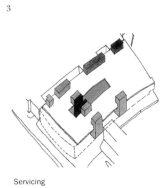
Environmental condition

3

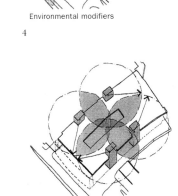
Environmental modifiers

4

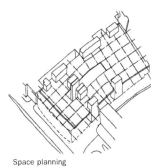
Atrium

5

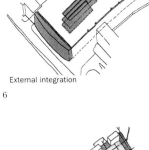
External integration

6

Servicing

7

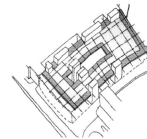
Life safety

8

Space planning

9

Space planning

10

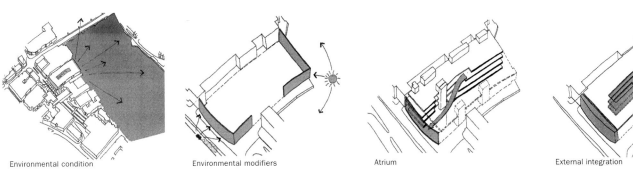

11

12

13

1   Site plan
2   View of Upper Thames Street elevation showing entrance foyer behind curved glass wall
3–10   Analysis diagrams
11   Model cross-section showing internal public spaces
12   Atrium looking north
13   North bank of River Thames

14

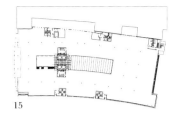

15

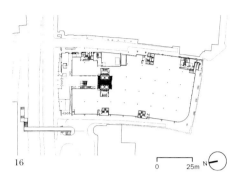

16

14 View from new footbridge over Upper Thames Street
15 Typical floor plan
16 Ground floor plan
17 Queenhithe Street elevation
18 Longitudinal section

19 Glass lift shaft and bridges at the center of the building, hung from a truss to allow a column-free dealer floor
20 Lift landing showing glass-clad lift shafts and translucent glass floors supported by castings
21 Study model of cantilevered river stairs
22 Corridor view

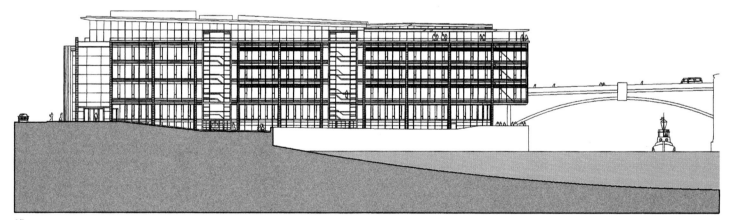

17

18

19

20

21

22

Kingdom Trade Center

Competition 1996
Riyadh, Saudi Arabia
100,000 square meters
Steel frame

The Kingdom Trade Center accommodates a range of residential, hotel, and office functions in a (985-foot) tower in the center of Riyadh.

In response to the extreme climate of Saudi Arabia, where summer temperatures are often above 40°C, the building is organized around a series of shaded internal garden spaces. These atria provide visual relief from the glare of the external environment and are a communal focus for building users. Service risers and elevators are set in three perimeter masts that provide the structure's primary support.

KPFI, London

1   Detail of tower top (services, primary structure, and vertical circulation are organized in three external masts at the building's perimeter)
2   Tower section
3   Kingdom offices
4   Offices
5   Hotel
6   Garden spaces

1

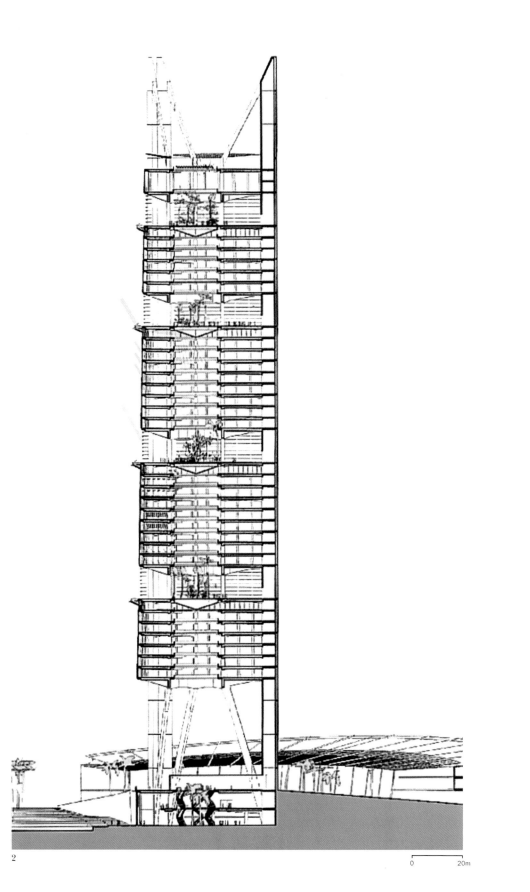

2

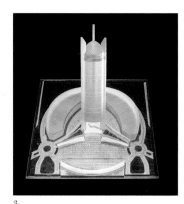

3

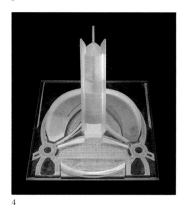

4

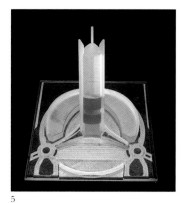

5

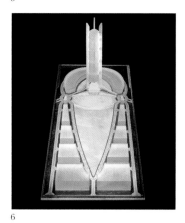

6

0   20m

Centre International Rogier

Design/Completion 1994/2000
Brussels, Belgium
59,000 square meters
Steel composite with concrete cores
Glass, aluminum

The Centre International Rogier was
originally constructed in an avante-garde
spirit in 1959 as a multi-use complex it
contained two theaters, a conference
center, offices, apartments, and retail
units. It was the first high-rise in Brussels
and, when constructed, was the tallest
building in Belgium.

The brief for the renovation of the
building called for the replacement of the
residential and low-grade offices with high-
grade flexible office space, while retaining
the theaters and upgrading the retail
space. A detailed technical analysis of the
existing structure concluded that a small-
scale renovation was both technically and
commercially unfeasable, and that the
tower portion of the building should
therefore be completely demolished and
reconstructed.

The new steel structure is supported by
existing concrete columns which pass
through the retained theater and, as a
result, the new scheme retains the same
plan as the original building.

Planning restrictions and the desire
to maximize the building's surface area
forced extremely low floor-to-floor

Continued

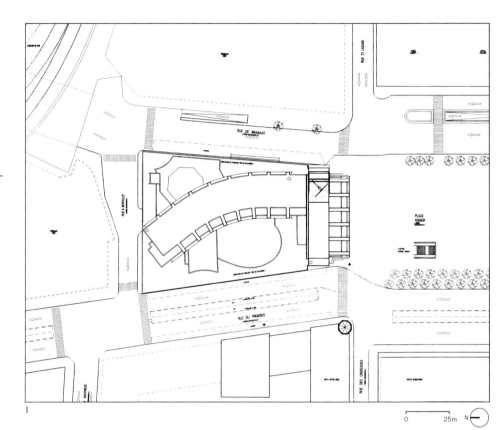

1

0   25m   N

1   Site plan
2   Existing building
Opposite:
    Model view looking towards main facade

2

196

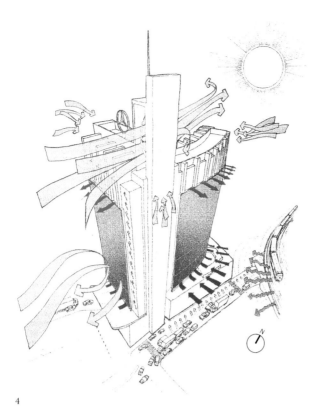

4

5

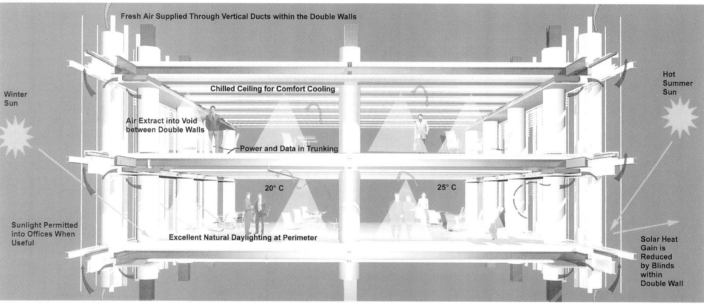

Fresh Air Supplied Through Vertical Ducts within the Double Walls

Winter Sun

Chilled Ceiling for Comfort Cooling

Air Extract into Void between Double Walls

Power and Data in Trunking

20° C

25° C

Excellent Natural Daylighting at Perimeter

Sunlight Permitted into Offices When Useful

Hot Summer Sun

Solar Heat Gain is Reduced by Blinds within Double Wall

6

7

heights. The development of a perimeter servicing strategy avoided the need for primary services to pass between floors, thereby minimizing ceiling depth.

The main facades are fully glazed double-skin thermal flues which contain the main air supply ducts and act as air return plenums. This construction creates an extremely efficient thermal buffer around the offices. Roof-mounted wind turbines contribute to the building's electrical supply.

KPFI, London

4   Diagram of environmental generators
5   Axonometric diagram of double wall and electrical and air distribution
6   Section of typical floor showing natural and environmental systems
7   Model view of double wall
8   Model view from north

8

Bismarckstrasse 101

Design/Completion 1992/1994
Berlin-Charlottenburg, Germany
Fèrinel Deutschland GmbH
6,500 square meters
Concrete frame and folded concrete wall
Plastered concrete, patinated brass, white marble, glass,
powder-coated aluminum

This five-story office building occupies
a corner site on Bismarckstrasse, a modern
thoroughfare in west Berlin. A sinuous
curve which develops out of the adjacent
building unifies the side and front
elevations, giving the building great
prominence on the main street. On the
courtyard side, planted terraces step down
toward the neighboring residences.

French doors in the glass facade provide
fresh air to offices. The environmental
strategy incorporates external sunshading,
underfloor cooled ventilation, operable
windows, floor-standing uplights, and
an exposed concrete ceiling for thermal
storage.

KPFI, London

1

2

1 Bismarckstrasse
2 Bismarckstrasse entrance
3&4 Facade details
5 Weimarstrasse elevation

3

4

5

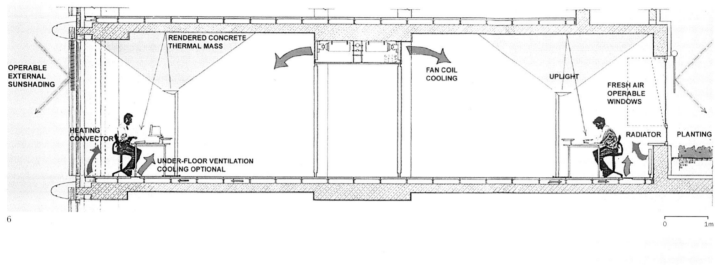

6

7

8

9

Provinciehuis

Design/Completion 1994/1998
The Hague, The Netherlands
24,000 square meters (new building)
20,000 square meters (renovation)
In-situ concrete flat slab construction
Brick, clear glass, white aluminum, stainless steel

The Province of South Holland sought an addition to the Statenzaal, the seat of the regional government. The existing buildings and the new additions are on a prominent site on the corner of The Hague's major park, the Malieveld.

The site suggested a strategy of two building types: to the rear, a taller slab which would act as a backdrop, and in the front, a lower L-shaped building attached to the existing Province Hall, Statenzaal. Together, these buildings create an inner courtyard. At the point where the two structures might have touched, they are instead held back, almost as if recoiling from each other. The result is a wide entrance which welcomes pedestrians approaching from the city centre.

The facade along the main street derives from the dynamic character of the building form and from the conventions of early 20th century Dutch architecture. Strip windows set between horizontal bands of brick are modulated by the dynamic rhythm of operable windows.

KPFI, London

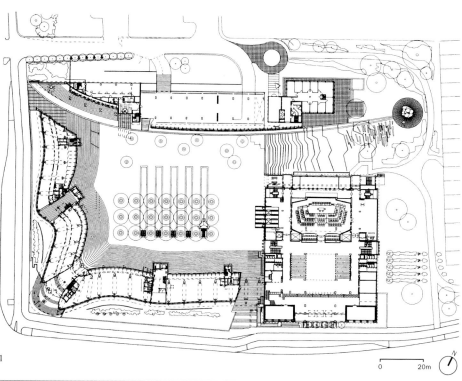

1

0   20m

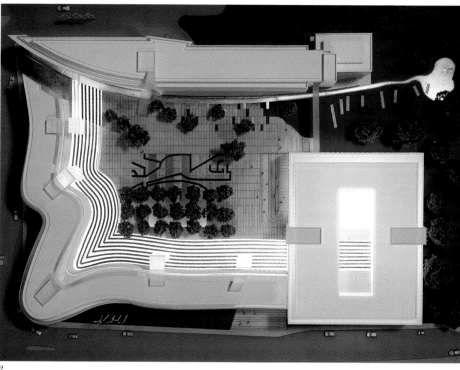

2

1 Ground floor level including restaurant, cafe,
  and exhibition area
2 Plan view
3 Aerial view of model looking west

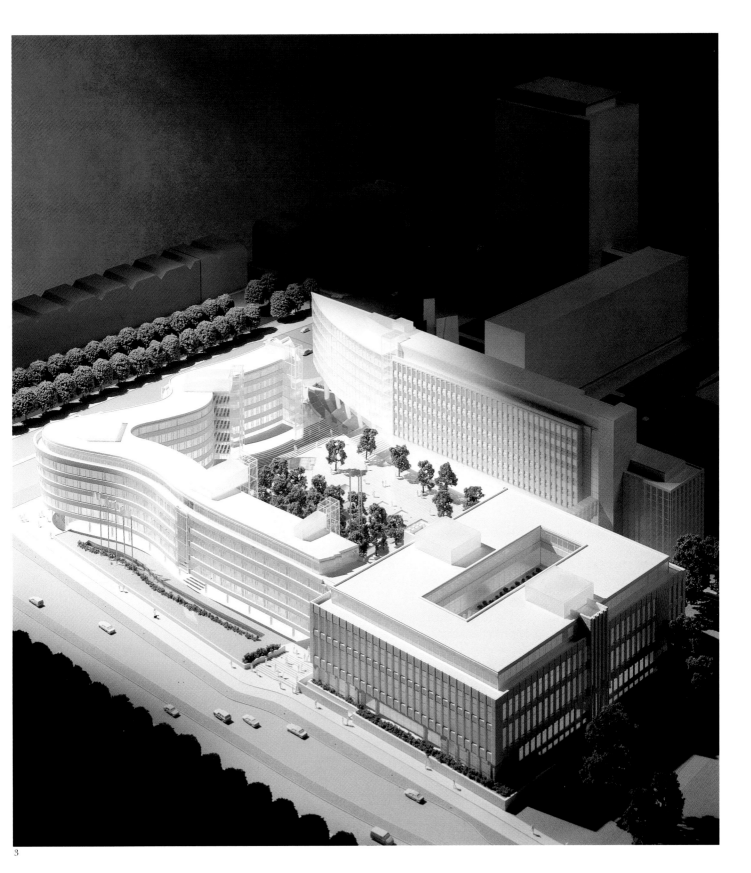

3

4

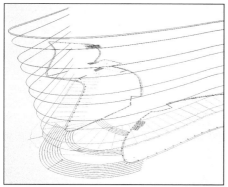

5

6

4   Bend at street corner
5   Diagram of bend at corner
6   View of elevator lobby
7   Plan of bend at corner
8   Existing paving pattern inside Statenzaal
9   Detail of corner
10 Courtyard entry
11 Partial aerial including courtyard
12 City lights at night

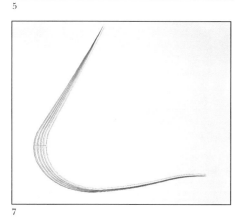

7

8

9

10

11

12

Opel Kreisel

Design/Completion 1995/2000
Frankfurt am Main, Germany
Immo THA Verwaltungs GmbH & Co. Immobilien KG
25,453 square meters (gross floor area)
Reinforced concrete construction
Clear glass curtainwall with partially integrated photovoltaic areas,
fair-faced concrete, wire mesh

Opel Kreisel is the gateway to Theodor-Heuss-Allee, the western arterial road which connects Frankfurt am Main's trade fairgrounds to the city center.

The tower's dynamic stepping shape serves as a gateway into Frankfurt am Main. Its office floors cantilever from the core and float 11 meters above the ground floor entrance lobby. Floor-to-ceiling clear glass allows expansive views. Operable windows behind perforated metal sunscreens occur in every second planning module, breaking the typical modular rhythm.

A lower pavilion building contains a large-span, column-free trading floor, benefiting from large, skylit ceiling coffers. A garden and small lake create a buffer to the busy highway. An L-shaped office zone surrounds the pavilion on two sides, its orthogonal form chosen to maintain the urban structure established by neighboring buildings.

Photovoltaic cells cover the entire high-rise core, facades, and roof to reduce fossil fuel consumption.

KPFI, London

1

208

1   East elevation looking northwest
2   West–east section
3   First floor with trading areas
4   Typical floor plan
5   Site plan
6   East elevation showing main entrance to the tower

2

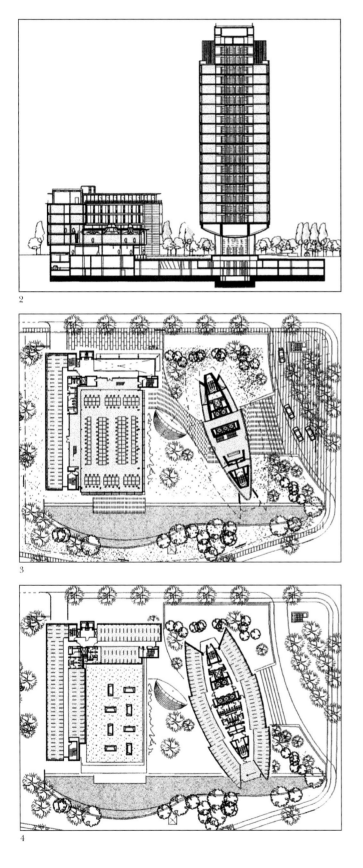

3

4

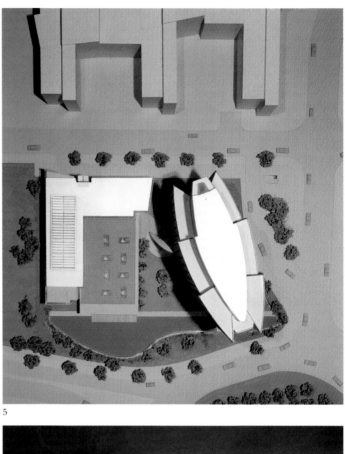

5

6

Forum Frankfurt

Design/Completion 1988/1997
Frankfurt am Main, Germany
Dinara BV and Egge Mountains BV
77,000 square meters (gross floor area)
Concrete frame
Metal and glass cladding, extensive use of natural stone

These two towers are situated next to the new Frankfurt exhibition hall on the northwestern edge of the city. The 223-foot space between the towers is designed as a simple, green urban plaza.

The outer facades are curved to suggest that each is part of a greater whole that has been split apart. The curved volumes have opaque facades with strongly articulated vertical fins. The inner facades are horizontal, suggesting a more delicate, transparent inner layer.

KPFI, London

1

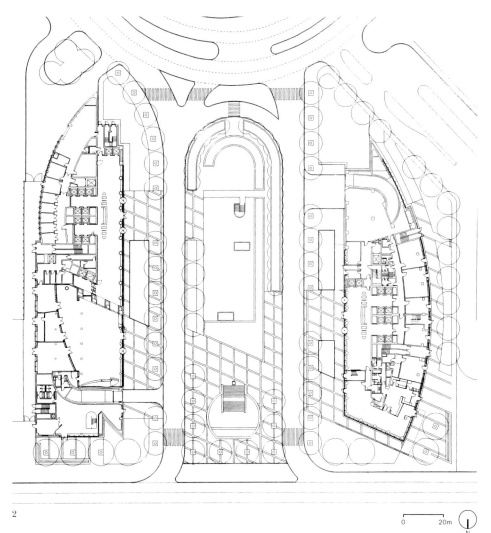

1　Kastor and Pollux from the old marshing yards which are part of the masterplan
2　Site plan
3　View from southwest
4　Detail of Kastor's southern edge
5　The vertically-accentuated (outwards) facade of Pollux
6　Interior view of atrium with gallery stairs and waterwall
7　The horizontally-articulated (inward) facade of Kastor

2

0　　　20m

N

3

4

5

6

7

Wave Tower

Design/Completion 1995/1998
Bangkok, Thailand
Wave Development Limited
49,000 square meters (gross floor area)
In-situ reinforced concrete utilizing high-strength
and post-tension technology
Clear silver glass and white aluminum

In Bangkok, buildings must be set back
from the property line behind a sloping
line drawn from the opposite side of the
street. One of the challenges of building
in the city is to make this sloping plane
appear to be a natural result of the
building form.

The plan of Wave Tower is simple: two
half ellipses are slightly shifted against
each other. The offset between the two
halves allows fresh air to be introduced
to the mechanical room at each floor.
At the top the two forms peel apart,
revealing the building's skeletal concrete
frame. The result is a dynamic silhouette
on the Bangkok skyline.

Each curve is clad in a simple curtainwall
of different density. The resulting light
filigree patterning is reminiscent of Thai
basketry.

KPFI London

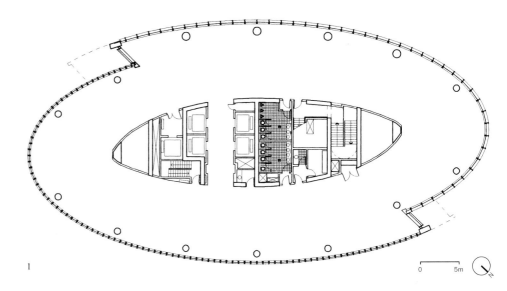

1

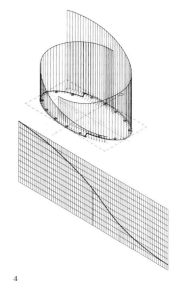

3

1 Typical floor plan
2 Front elevation
3 Detail of tower top
4 Diagram of unwrapping top of building
Opposite:
    Side elevation

2   4

Wave-Sathorn Financial Tower

Design/Completion 1996/1999
Bangkok, Thailand
Wave Development Limited
60,000 square meters (gross floor area)
In-situ reinforced concrete utilizing high-strength and post-tension
technology
Clear silver glass, white aluminum

The Sathorn Road project in Bangkok
is a further development of ideas first
investigated in Wave Tower. Here,
however, the building is on a corner site
and thus two set back angles applied.
In addition, the client requested a larger
floor plate.

The plan is curved around three sides and
on the fourth is sliced to reveal the zones
of office, core, and office. A simple vertical
curtainwall wraps around the curve, while
the cut section is clad with a more
articulated horizontal fabric.

KPFI, London

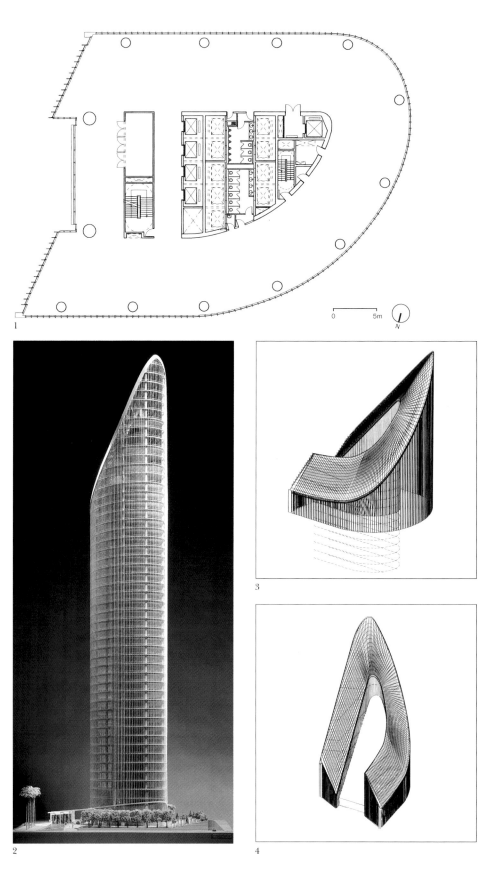

1   Typical low-rise office floor plan
2   Side elevation of model
3&4   Axonometric of top of tower
Opposite:
      Front elevation

Wave House

Design/Completion 1996/2000
Bangkok, Thailand
Wave Development Limited
55,000 square meters (gross floor area)
In-situ reinforced concrete
Clear silver glass, white aluminum

The Wave House project is the third in the series of buildings designed for Bangkok. The site is located on Sukhumvit, an important commercial street which diagonally intersects with the orthogonal city grid. The resulting site is trapezoidal in shape and the plan takes the form of two slightly bent walls slipped past each other.

The building top, canted once again to follow the setback line, suggests a movement to the street. The realigned elevation now affords expansive vistas to the city's growing financial centre.

KPFI, London

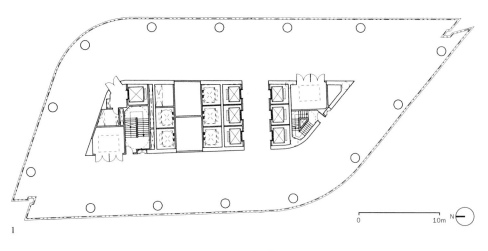

1

1 Site plan
2 View up Sukhumvit Road
3 View down Sukhumvit Road
4 Front elevation

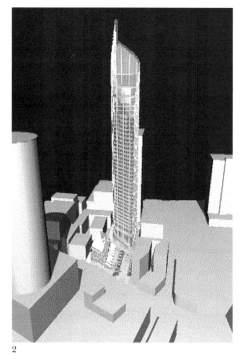

2

3

216

KBB

Design/Completion 1995/1999
Düsseldorf, Germany
Gedusham Properties BV
34,000 square meters (gross floor area)
Concrete, steel columns
Clear glass, sandblasted glass, anodized aluminum frames,
natural stone, birch panels, exposed plastered concrete

Located in Düsseldorf's financial district, KBB aims to provide a high-quality work environment with reduced energy consumption. A large-span glass roof membrane with interactive sunshading components covers an internal court which serves as a thermal buffer. Inside the court, planted terraces and fountains create a tranquil garden. The courtyard serves as the building's lungs, supplying fresh air to the offices.

A clear glass double-skin facade regulates heat gain, air flow, and daylight. The facade combines components of the larger module outer skin, the inner planning module, and irregularly placed frosted opening windows to create layered readings at multiple scales. Multi-story garden volumes, inserted at strategic perimeter points, identify the garden courtyard and mitigate the large block structure.

KPFI, London

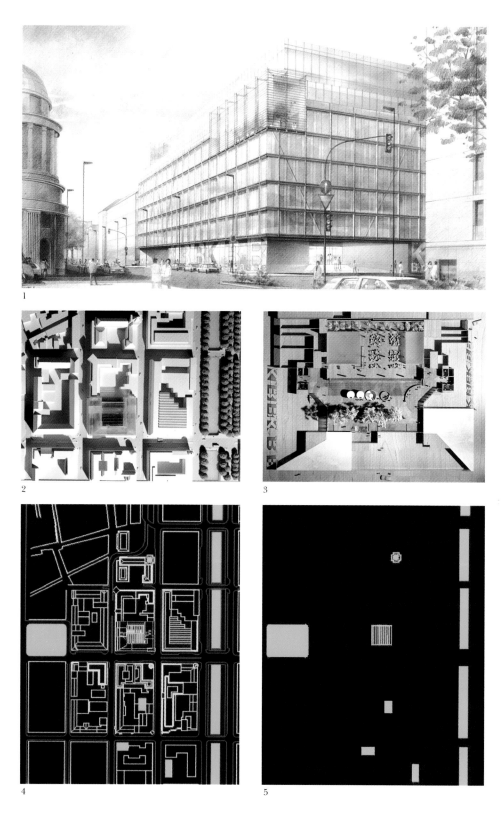

1

2

3

4

5

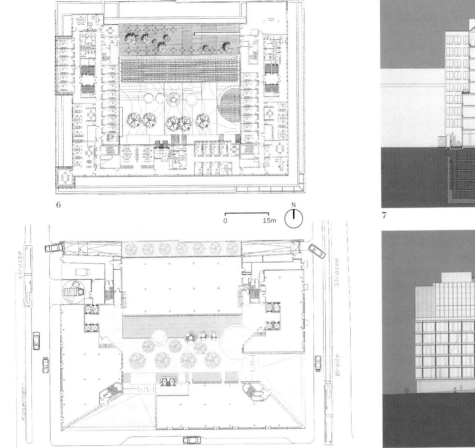

6

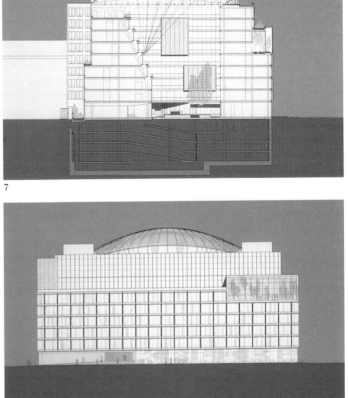

7

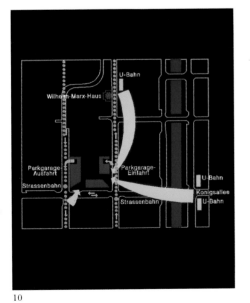

8

9

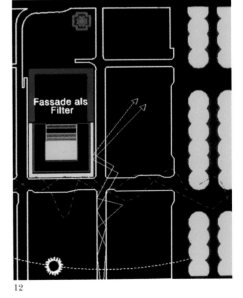

10

11

12

13

14

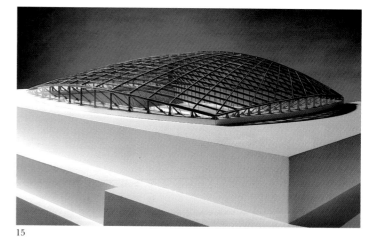

15

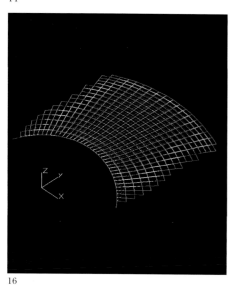

16

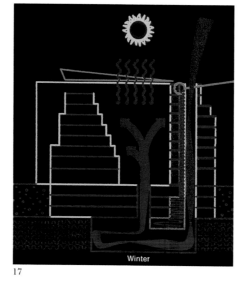

17

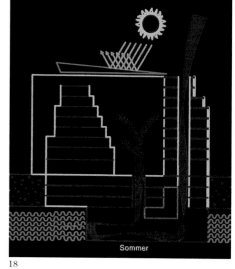

18

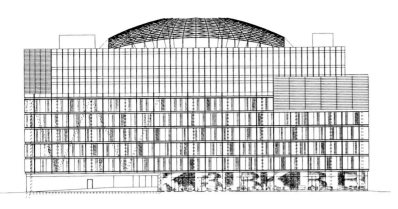

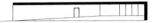

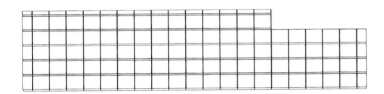

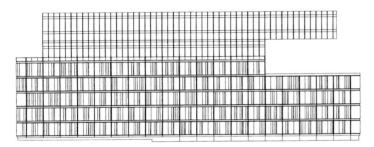

19

20

21

22

23

Daelim International Headquarters

Competition 1996
Seoul, Korea
Daelim Industrial Company Limited
76,000 square meters (offices)
38,000 square meters (condominiums)
22,000 square meters (retail/sports/financial)
62,000 square meters (parking)
Steel frame, structural tube technology
Clear glass, bronze

The parti for the Daelim Headquarters
proposal is simple: two rectangular wings
are pried open to bring light to both sides
of the floor plate, to orient the building
towards the hills beyond, and to form a
focal point for the entire company. Glass
bridges and glass lifts in open frameworks
animate the atrium.

The long north and south faces of the
building are double walls incorporating
the structural tube. Photovoltaic cells at
the top of the building act both as energy
collectors and as sunshades for the atrium.

A separate condominium building and
below-grade retail/sports structure
complete the composition. The ground
floor of the entire site is left open,
allowing the landscape to flow into
the building.

KPFI, London

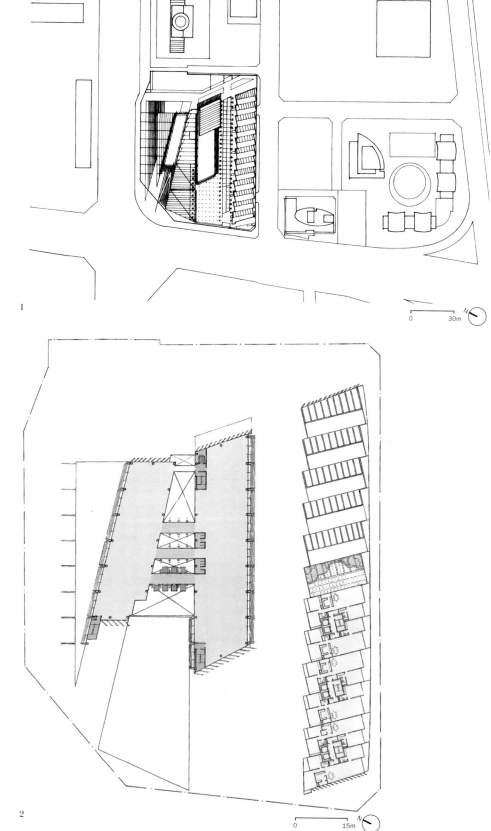

1

1 Site plan
2 Typical floor plan
Opposite:
   Front elevation

2

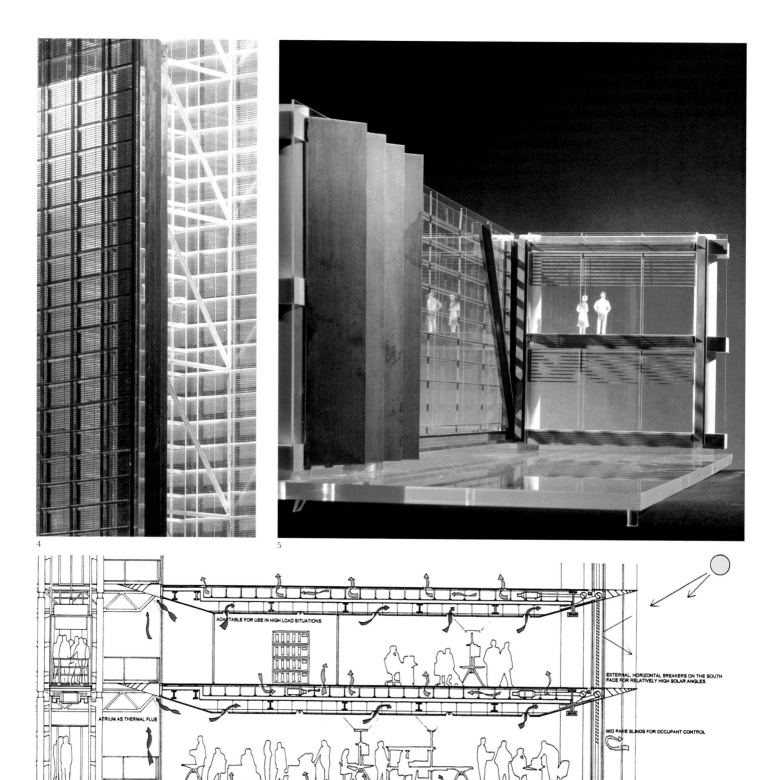

4

5

6

ADAPTABLE FOR USE IN HIGH LOAD SITUATIONS.

ATRIUM AS THERMAL FLUE

EXTERNAL, HORIZONTAL BREAKERS ON THE SOUTH FACE FOR RELATIVELY HIGH SOLAR ANGLES.

MID PANE BLINDS FOR OCCUPANT CONTROL

INTEGRATES WELL WITH ELECTRICAL AND IT SERVICES. BUILDING SERVICES STRATEGY

7

0   15m

8

Coolsingel

Design/Completion 1996
Rotterdam, The Netherlands
Boufonds BV/City of Rotterdam (joint venture)
35,000 square meters (office); 10,000 square meters
(theatre, restaurant, retail)
In-situ reinforced concrete
Clear glass in a thermal wall system, bronze, marble, maple wood

The new building sits behind a low-rise
post-war structure which will be preserved.
The parti is the same as for Daelim
Headquarters, but here the similarity
rather than the differences between the
inner and outer walls are stressed.
A continuous ribbon of glass wraps around
the offices. Once again, glass bridges and
glass lifts in open framework animate the
atrium.

The outer glass wall of the atrium slopes
in section. As it falls to the street, the glass
wall breaks through the existing facades
to form the building entry.

KPFI, London

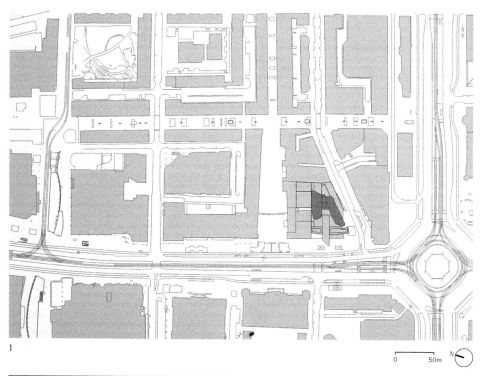

1

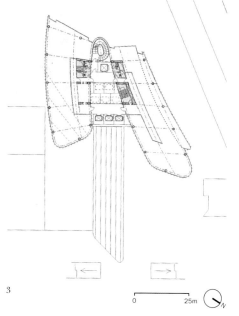

0   50m

3

0   25m

2

1   Location map
2   West elevation
3   Typical low-rise plan
Opposite:
    View from Coolsingel

Oxford Institute for American Studies

Design/Completion 1994/1998
Oxford, England
Oxford University
2,400 square meters
Concrete frame
Stone, bronze, glass, timber

The Institute for American Studies at Oxford will be a place of research, teaching, and discussion: a forum for the exchange of ideas between visitors, academics, and students. The scheme supports these aims by creating a building which is open and accessible, clear in its organization, and welcoming to its users.

The proposal arranges the accommodation in a compact pavilion addressing the re-landscaped Mansfield College gardens. The library, which is to house the important collection at present held in Rhodes House, is at the heart of the building design. Its reading room, a lofty, light-filled volume overlooking the garden, serves both to identify the institute to the outside world and to provide a focus for the life within the building.

KPFI, London

1

2

0   5m   N

1 Reading room from the study gallery
2 Site plan: aerial view
3 The institute seen from Mansfield College
  principal's garden

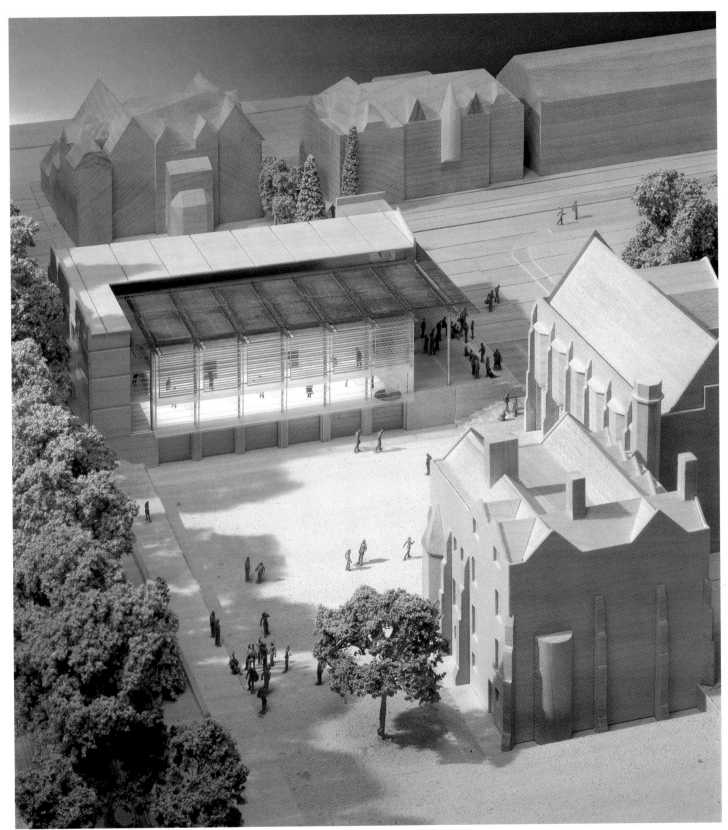

3

4

5

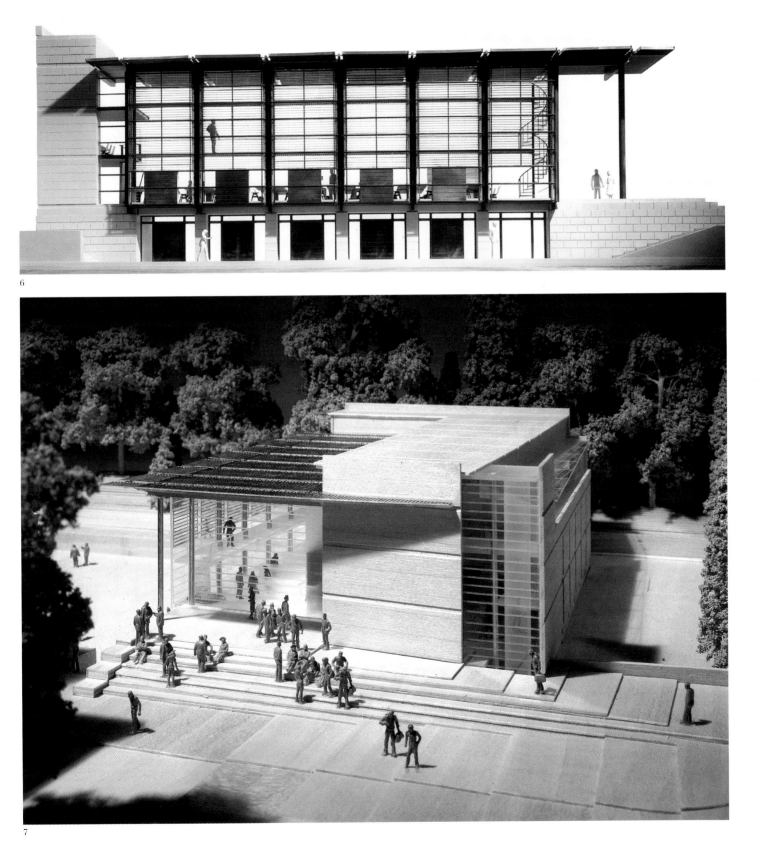

6

7

FIRM PROFILE

Biographies

A. Eugene Kohn FAIA, RIBA, JIA
Principal

It was in 1976, along with William Pedersen and Sheldon Fox, that A. Eugene Kohn founded Kohn Pedersen Fox Associates PC, a firm of architects and planners committed to the principle of design excellence. Since then, Mr Kohn has served as Partner-in-Charge of many of Kohn Pedersen Fox's major domestic and international projects and is responsible for many of the firm's new commissions. He contributes to each Kohn Pedersen Fox design, from corporate headquarters and office buildings to hotels and institutional facilities.

A. Eugene Kohn is respected worldwide, not only for his 40-year career as an architect, but also for his inspirational leadership qualities. As founder and Principal of Kohn Pedersen Fox, he has developed a global strategy and has shaped the firm into one of the world's leaders in all aspects of architecture. KPF is reknowned for buildings which are sensitive to their context and which establish a unique and memorable image on the exterior, while creating work environments on the interior which reinforce the clients' overall mission and function. In an article published in September 1991, *Architecture* asked its readers: "Of today's practicing architects, whose work do you admire?" Kohn Pedersen Fox Associates tied for first place and were cited for their "principled and intelligent" approach to design. In 1990 KPF was honored with the prestigious AIA Architectural Firm Award—the youngest firm ever to receive this one-time award. Three projects for which Mr Kohn has been Partner-in-Charge have won National AIA Design Awards: 333 Wacker Drive, Chicago; Procter & Gamble Headquarters, Cincinnati, Ohio; and DG Bank Headquarters, Frankfurt, Germany.

Prior to founding Kohn Pedersen Fox Associates in 1976, Mr Kohn was President and Partner of John Carl Warnecke and Associates (1967–76); Design Director of Welton Becket Associates New York (1965–67); and Senior Designer at Vincent G. Kling Associates in Philadelphia, Pennsylvania (1960–65), where two of his designs received AIA National Honor Awards. Mr Kohn served as an officer in the US Navy, retiring as Lieutenant Commander after three years active duty (1953–56) and five years reserve duty.

Mr Kohn was honored in 1987 by the National Education Fund and in 1995 by the Sheltering Arms Children Service. In 1996 Mr Kohn was honored with the Sidney L. Strauss Award from the New York Society of Architects, and in 1997 with the Lifetime Achievement Award given by the Wharton Real Estate Center.

Mr Kohn is registered as an architect in 26 states, as well as in Great Britain and Japan. He is a Fellow of the American Institute of Architects and a member of its Octagon Society. During 1988 Mr Kohn held the position of President of the AIA New York City

Chapter. He is also a member of the Royal Institute of British Architects and the Japan Institute of Architects, and an honorary Fellow of the Philippine Institute of Architects.

He has served on the boards of directors of the Architectural League and the Chicago City Ballet, as well as on the advisory board for the Master of Science degree in Real Estate Development at Columbia University's Graduate School of Architecture, Planning, and Preservation, and on the Yale University Committee on the Art Gallery and British Arts Center. Mr Kohn also served as a Trustee for the University of Pennsylvania and currently serves on the Board of Overseers at the University of Pennsylvania's Graduate School of Fine Arts, and the Wharton Real Estate Center Advisory Board. In addition, he is a member of the Board of the National Realty Committee, the Museum for African Art of New York, the Silvermine Art Guild, and the Board of Sheltering Arms Children Service, and is a Trustee for the Urban Land Institute.

Mr Kohn has lectured extensively on the subject of contemporary architecture and has been invited to participate in conferences throughout the world, including the Second Asian Congress of Architects in Kuala Lumpur, Malaysia, as keynote speaker. He was keynote speaker at the 1997 National Philippine AIA convention in Manila. He has delivered keynote speeches to professional associations, civic and educational organizations, and industry and trade groups in Los Angeles, Dallas, Chicago, Washington, DC, and New York; London; Hong Kong; Nagoya, Osaka, and Tokyo in Japan; Sydney, Brisbane, Melbourne, and Perth in Australia; and Wellington, New Zealand. He also spoke in several cities in the former Soviet Union on behalf of the United States Information Agency.

Mr Kohn has served as chairman of design award juries for the State of California AIA, North Carolina AIA, the city of Denver AIA, and the city of Pittsburgh AIA, and as a juror for the Urban Land Institute awards program. In addition, he has lectured numerous times at AIA chapters nationwide. As a visiting critic and guest lecturer, Mr Kohn has also appeared at Bucknell, Harvard, UCLA, University of Pennsylvania, Penn State, University of Kentucky, University of Tennessee, Clemson University, the University of Wisconsin, and Yale University. For the last six years Mr Kohn has conducted and taught courses during the summer program at the Harvard University Graduate School of Design on marketing, presentation skills, and office buildings. Mr Kohn's architectural articles have been published in the United States and abroad, and he has contributed chapters for several architectural books.

Mr Kohn received his Bachelor of Architecture degree in 1953 and his Master of Architecture degree in 1957, both from the University of Pennsylvania, where he was Theopolis Parsons Chandler Graduate Fellow. In 1982 he completed the Real Estate Development Course at Harvard University's Graduate School of Design.

William Pedersen FAIA
Principal

William Pedersen received a Bachelor of Architecture degree from the University of Minnesota in 1961 and was a recipient of the school's Gargoyle Club Prize. In 1963 he received a Master of Architecture degree from the Massachusetts Institute of Technology, where he was a Whitney Fellow. In 1966 he won the Rome Prize in Architecture and studied for two years at the American Academy in Rome.

Mr Pedersen has received numerous design awards for his work at Kohn Pedersen Fox, the firm he co-founded in 1976. These include the 1990 AIA Architectural Firm Award and three National AIA Honor Awards for Westendstrasse 1, Frankfurt, Germany (1994); Procter & Gamble World Headquarters, Cincinnati, Ohio (1987); and 333 Wacker Drive, Chicago, Illinois (1984). He has also received the *Progressive Architecture* Design Award for Station Center in White Plains, New York (1987); Mainzer Landstrasse 58 in Frankfurt, Germany (1988); Rockefeller Plaza West in New York City (1989); and the Rodin Museum at Samsung Plaza, Seoul, Korea (1996); as well as a Design Citation for The World Bank in Washington, DC (1990) and the Distinguished Architecture Award for 1250 Boulevard René-Lévesque in Montreal, Canada (1993).

Mr Pedersen has also published several articles including: "Considerations for Urban Architecture and the Tall Building" in *Southwest Center: The Houston Competition* (Rizzoli International, 1983); "Methods & Intentions 1976–1989" in *Process: Architecture* (1989); "The Bow and the Lyre" in *Kohn Pedersen Fox: Architecture and Urbanism 1986–1992* (Rizzoli International, 1993); and "Strategies for the Design of Tall Buildings" in *A+U* (June 1996).

Mr Pedersen has been a visiting critic at the Rhode Island School of Design (1982), Columbia University (1983), and Harvard University (1984), and has held the Eero Saarinen Chair at Yale University (1986). In addition, he has been honored as the Herbert S. Greenward Distinguished Professor in Architecture at the University of Illinois at Chicago (1989).

Mr Pedersen is a Fellow of the American Institute of Architects and of the American Academy in Rome. He has also received the 1985 Arnold Brunner Memorial Prize in Architecture from the American Academy and the Institute of Arts and Letters "for his contributions to architecture as an art."

Robert L. Cioppa FAIA
Principal

Robert L. Cioppa has more than 30 years
of experience as an architect and
administrator. He has been the Managing
Principal for the design and construction
of government, corporate headquarters,
and investment office buildings totaling
more than $1 billion, for such clients as the United States General
Services Administration, the Urban Investment and Development
Company, INA Corporation, Reliance Development Group,
Prudential Insurance Company of America, Procter & Gamble,
General Mills, Lincoln Properties, First Boston, Shearson
Lehman/E.F. Hutton, Rockefeller Development Corporation,
St Paul Companies, Stanford University, and Capital Cities/ABC.

In 1979, three years after joining Kohn Pedersen Fox, Mr Cioppa
was asked to become a Principal of the firm and assumed primary
responsibility for the management of major projects. In 1995,
upon the retirement of Sheldon Fox, he undertook responsibility
for the administration of financial operations for KPF.

Many of the projects for which Mr Cioppa has served as Managing
Principal have received national and international recognition
and awards for their design and execution. These awards include:
the New York City and the New York State AIA Distinguished
Design Award for the ABC Television Studios 23/24, and the New
York City Bard Award for the ABC Armory, both in New York City;
the New York Chapter AIA Distinguished Design Award for One
Logan Square in Philadelphia, Pennsylvania; the Washington, DC
Chapter AIA Excellence in Design Award for the Washington
News Bureau; the Philadelphia Chapter AIA Design Award for
Eight Penn Center in Philadelphia, Pennsylvania; a National AIA
Design Award for the Proctor & Gamble Headquarters in
Cincinnati, Ohio; and three GSA Design Awards for the US
courthouses in Portland, Oregon, Foley Square, New York, and
Minneapolis, Minnesota.

Mr Cioppa received his Bachelor of Architecture degree from
Pratt Institute in 1967 and in 1983 graduated from the Stanford
University Graduate School of Business Executive Program.
Mr Cioppa is a Fellow of the American Institute of Architects.

William C. Louie FAIA
Principal

William C. Louie joined Kohn Pedersen Fox in 1977, a year after its inception, and became a prime contributor to the body of work that has earned the firm design recognition, including the prestigious 1990 AIA Architectural Firm Award. With 35 years of experience as an architect, he has honed his craft in all aspects of the profession. Since 1984 he has served as a Design Partner on projects which account for more than $1.8 billion of new construction. He led the practice overseas with projects now in Australia, Lebanon, Indonesia, China, Singapore, Korea, Malaysia, Taiwan, and Hong Kong, in addition to his work throughout the United States.

In 1986 he won the New York State AIA Merit Award for General Re Corporation Headquarters in Stamford, Connecticut, and in 1990, the AIA Excellence in Design Award for 1325 Avenue of the Americas in New York City. In 1988 he won the coveted NAIOP Grand Award for Arbor Circle North & South in Parsippany, New Jersey. For his creative use of precast concrete he won three Design Awards in 1984, 1986, and 1990 for Goldome Bank Headquarters, Arbor Circle North & South, and Shearson Lehman Hutton Plaza respectively. For their innovative integration of engineering solutions, three of his projects received Certificate of Engineering Excellence citations: Mellon Bank Center and Shearson Lehman Hutton Plaza in 1991 and Chifley Tower in 1993. More recently, Mr Louie won the 1996 GSA Design Honors Award for Building Design Excellence for the US Courthouse at Foley Square in New York City.

Some of his more recent commissions include: Bank Niaga Headquarters in Jakarta, Indonesia; Singapore Exchange Center (to house the Mercantile and Stock Exchanges) in Singapore; Hong Kong Electric Headquarters in Hong Kong; Plaza 66, a 2.5-million-square-foot office and retail complex in Shanghai, China; Taichung Tower, a hotel and condominium tower in Taichung, Taiwan; Yuksomdong, a retail office building, and Seocho Fashion Center, both in Seoul, Korea; Rue Foch Building, an office and retail structure in Beirut, Lebanon; and Menara Mulpha Headquarters in Kuala Lumpur, Malaysia.

Mr Louie received his Bachelor of Science in Architecture degree from the City College of New York in 1974. He has been a guest lecturer to architects in various cities in Asia and has served on design juries. He was featured in the October 1996 issue of *B International* magazine and was selected as one of the 500 most influential Asian Americans in the 1996 inaugural issue of *Avenue Asia* magazine and again in the 1997 issue. He is a member of the New York State Association of Architects and a Fellow of the American Institute of Architects.

Lee A. Polisano AIA, RIBA, Dipl.-Ing.
Principal

Lee A. Polisano was born in Atlantic City, New Jersey, and received his Master of Architecture degree at the Virginia Polytechnic Institute. He joined Kohn Pedersen Fox in 1981, became a Partner in 1986, and in 1989 co-founded Kohn Pedersen Fox International in London, where he is the Senior Partner-in-Charge and has overall management responsibility.

Mr Polisano's work, which involves the integration of building design and technology, leads Kohn Pedersen Fox's research and development of environmentally responsive buildings. Previously he has been honored by *Engineering News Record* and the US construction industry for his building design and development of construction techniques using architectural concrete. His current projects include the Thames Court building in London and the innovative KBB development in Düsseldorf, Germany.

Mr Polisano has published several articles, including "Complexity and Contrast—American and European High-Rise Buildings" in *Architectural Design* (1995), and he is frequently invited to address academic and professional symposia, such as the World Conference on Tall Buildings and Urban Habitat in (Amsterdam 1995) and the Royal Institute of Architects National Convention (Scotland 1995) and The Intelligent Building Symposium (Stuttgart 1996).

Mr Polisano is a member of the American Institute of Architects, the Royal Institute of British Architects, and the Architektenkammer Berlin.

David M. Leventhal AIA
Principal

David Leventhal is a Senior Partner of Kohn Pedersen Fox Associates PC and is Partner-in-Charge of Design for the London office. A member of the firm for 18 years, he has been the designer of numerous office, institutional, master plan, and residential schemes. Recently he was the Design Partner of the winning competition entries for the headquarters of the Province of South Holland, the Institute for American Studies at Oxford University, and the new Parliament House in Nicosia, Cyprus. He designed the Chicago Title Center, a 50-story office and retail complex. The drawings of this scheme served as the logo for "Chicago Architecture Today," an exhibition which toured the United States.

In Brussels he is working on the design of the Martini Tower, a low-energy high-rise building which includes a thermally sensitive wall and wind generators; in Bangkok he has designed three high-rises, now under construction. The Heron International building in New York City, an office building in midtown Manhattan, won the 1988 New York AIA Design Award. In March 1995 the work of KPF's London office was featured as the cover story of *World Architecture*.

Mr Leventhal received his Bachelor of Arts and Master of Architecture degrees from Harvard University. He has exhibited and lectured at the Chicago Architectural Center, the University of Delft, the Royal Academy in London, and Harvard University. He is also a member of the Collections Committee of the Fogg Art Museum at Harvard.

Gregory Clement AIA
Principal

Gregory Clement was born in Providence, Rhode Island, in 1950. He received a Bachelor of Arts degree in 1973 and a Master of Architecture degree in 1975, both from the University of Pennsylvania in Philadelphia. He was also the recipient of the Dales Traveling Fellowship in 1974 as well as other merit scholarships while at the University of Pennsylvania.

Prior to joining Kohn Pedersen Fox in 1984, Mr Clement was a Senior Designer at I.M. Pei & Partners in New York City (1982–84) and an Associate at Cathers, Lukens, Thompson in Philadelphia (1980–82), where he was responsible for the Philadelphia College of Art expansion and restoration, which received an honorable mention from the Philadelphia Chapter of the AIA in 1982. He was also affiliated with Geddes Brecher Qualls Cunningham in Philadelphia, Pennsylvania, and Princeton, New Jersey (1976–78).

Since 1993, as a Partner at Kohn Pedersen Fox, Mr Clement has been responsible for the management of major projects across the United States, Europe, and Asia, as well as for the administration and operations of the firm in New York. Three of the projects he has worked on have received awards: Rockefeller Plaza West received the *Progressive Architecture* Design Citation in 1989; the Capital Cities/ABC Headquarters in New York City won the AIA/BIA Brick in Architecture Award in 1993; and the Rodin Museum at Samsung Center in Seoul, Korea, received an award from the New York City AIA and a *Progressive Architecture* Citation, both in 1996. Other projects for which he has been responsible include the Telecom Argentina Headquarters in Buenos Aires, Argentina; Warsaw Financial Center in Warsaw, Poland; and renovations to 55 Water Street in New York City. Currently, he is the Project Principal for the IBM Corporate Headquarters in Armonk, New York and a new academic facility for the Wharton School at the University of Pennsylvania.

Mr Clement is a member of the American Institute of Architects and a registered architect in Pennsylvania, Delaware, Connecticut, and New York State. In addition, he has served on numerous university architectural design juries.

Michael Greene AIA

Principal

Michael Greene joined Kohn Pedersen Fox in 1985 to work on the 400-room Hyatt Regency in Old Greenwich, Connecticut, and Shearson Lehman Hutton Plaza in New York City.

He has been Project Manager for numerous projects, including Ninth Avenue Tower in New York City; Canary Wharf FC-6 in the docklands of London; the Nagoya Station Building in Nagoya and the Roppongi Towers in Tokyo, Japan; two resort hotel/casino projects planned for the Hainan Province of China; the Orchard Building in Singapore; a hotel/serviced apartment complex in Jakarta, Indonesia; and the Plaza Merdeka Master Plan in Kuala Lumpur, Malaysia.

Currently he is managing a 1.3-million-square-foot headquarters for Gannett Co. and USA Today, a 3.5-million-square-foot renovation of 55 Water Street in New York City, the Niaga II Office Tower in Jakarta, Indonesia, and the Singapore Exchange Centre.

Mr Greene received his Bachelor of Environmental Design degree in 1976 from North Carolina State University and his Master of Architecture in 1978 from Virginia Polytechnic Institute and State University. He is a registered architect in the State of North Carolina.

Paul Katz AIA

Principal

Paul Katz joined Kohn Pedersen Fox in 1984. In 1989 he was in charge of the competition-winning schemes for the Orlando City Hall in Florida and the Irvine Museum of Art in Orange County, California.

Besides working in various American and European cities, Mr Katz has primarily been responsible for projects in Asia, such as the Nagoya Station Building in Nagoya and the Tokyo Grand Hyatt, a hotel, office, and museum tower in downtown Tokyo, Japan; Nanjing Road mixed-use project and the Shanghai World Financial Center in Shanghai, China; 11 Chater Road, The Landmark retail center, and the Grand Centre, all in Hong Kong; the Esplanade Mall project in Singapore; and the Fort Bonifacio Landmark project, the ICEC Tower, and the First Metrobank Tower in Manila, the Philippines.

Before joining Kohn Pedersen Fox, Mr Katz worked for Michael Graves in Princeton, New Jersey. Mr Katz began his architectural studies at the University of Cape Town in South Africa and received a Bachelor of Architecture and Planning degree from the Israel Institute of Technology. He was awarded a Fellowship, and subsequently a Master of Architecture degree in 1984 from Princeton University, where he also taught design. Mr Katz has served as a guest critic at various universities, and as a visiting professor at the University of Notre Dame in South Bend, Indiana.

Kevin Kennon
Principal

Kevin Kennon joined Kohn Pedersen Fox in 1988, having trained in the offices of some of the country's most respected architects: I.M. Pei, Michael Graves, Kevin Roche and John Dinkeloo. His clients at Kohn Pedersen Fox over the last eight years include Samsung, Sony, Disney Development Company, Morgan Stanley, Federated Department Stores, Rockefeller Center Development Corporation, and Sotheby's.

He has received numerous awards, including project and honor awards from the New York City Chapter of the American Institute of Architects and a *Progressive Architecture* award for the Samsung Rodin Pavilion. He received a Young Architects Award from the Architectural League in 1992.

Mr Kennon has been visiting professor at Yale University (1988–92) and has lectured at Princeton and Rice Universities and the University of Houston.

Mr Kennon graduated from Amherst College with a Bachelor of Arts degree in 1980 and in 1984 received his Master of Architecture degree from Princeton University, where he was awarded the Thesis Prize. He is registered in the State of New York.

James von Klemperer AIA
Principal

James von Klemperer joined Kohn Pedersen Fox in 1984 and has since designed a series of major buildings, including the Bank Niaga Headquarters and the Niaga II Office Tower in Jakarta, Indonesia; the Yuksamdong mixed-use tower and the Dongbu Securities Headquarters in Seoul, Korea; and the Plaza 66 mixed-use project for Hang Lung in Shanghai, China. He has also designed a city for 10,000 people for the San Ju corporation on a 450-acre site south of Beijing, China.

In the United States, Mr von Klemperer was Senior Designer on the recently completed US Courthouse at Foley Square in New York City.

Mr von Klemperer graduated from Phillips Academy Andover in 1975, received a Bachelor of Arts degree from Harvard University in 1979, and a Master in Architecture degree from Princeton University in 1983. He also studied architecture at Trinity College in Cambridge, England, as a recipient of the Charles Henry Fiske Scholarship. He has lectured at Harvard University and has served on architecture juries at Princeton and Yale Universities.

Peter Schubert AIA
Principal

Peter Schubert joined Kohn Pedersen Fox in 1984 and has since worked on a wide variety of projects. He is currently Senior Designer for a mixed-use residential and office facility for Samyang in Seoul, South Korea, and a corporate headquarters for Posteel, also in Seoul. He is also the Senior Associate Design Partner for the First Hawaiian Bank Center in Honolulu, Hawaii, and the Atlanta Federal Center in Atlanta, Georgia.

Mr Schubert was among the Senior Designers working in collaboration on the winning competition entry for the World Bank Headquarters in Washington, DC. Other major competitions for which he was Senior Designer include the Singapore Arts Center, in Singapore, and an educational community for Disney in Osceola, Florida.

Prior to joining Kohn Pedersen Fox, Mr Schubert worked with Skidmore, Owings & Merrill, Peterson Littenberg, and Jon Michael Schwarting and Associates.

Mr Schubert graduated with a Bachelor of Science in Architecture degree in 1978 from Ohio State University, where he received the Alpha Rho Chi Medal for Outstanding Student Leadership and Academic Performance. He received his Master of Architecture degree in 1981 from Columbia University, where he was awarded the AIA Certificate for Outstanding Future Professionals.

Mr Schubert is a member of the Society for Historical Preservation and the American Institute of Architects.

Senior Associate Partners	Associate Partners
Alvarez, Tomas	Breen, Kieran
Bakker, Ron	Bushell, John
Blackman, Gabrielle	Dacosta, Glen
Chaiken, Joshua	Dörr, Gunter
Cook, Karen A.	Dunn, Dominic
Davis, J. William	Figliuzzi, Terri
Flanagan, Kevin	Gross, Peter
Goodwin, Robert	Hartwig, Robert
Hausler, Andreas	Hernandez, Tomas
Holzmann, Thomas	Hesselgren, Lars
Keeny, Christopher	Hocking, Doug
Koga, John	Long, David
Lerner, Jill	Lucas, John
Mosellie, Anthony	Min, Chulhong
Pilbrow, Fred	Nip, Bun-Wah
Smith, Jerri	Patterson, Russell
Waugh, Gregory	Reid, Duncan
Whitlock, Robert	Robison, Roger
	Sugiyama, Hisaya
	Tulkens, Bernard

Awards

Building Design Excellence Award
GSA Design Awards
US Courthouse
Foley Square, New York
1996

Building Design Excellence Citation
GSA Design Awards
US Courthouse
Minneapolis, Minnesota
1996

Design Award
44th Annual Progressive Architecture
Samsung Rodin Museum
Seoul, South Korea
1996

Project Design Award
New York Chapter AIA
Samsung Rodin Museum
Seoul, South Korea
1996

New Construction Building of the Year
Building Owners' and Managers'
Association New York Awards
US Courthouse
Foley Square, New York
1995–96

Project Honor Award
New York Chapter AIA
Greater Buffalo International Airport
New York, New York
1995

Project Design Award
New York Chapter AIA
Shanghai World Financial Center
Shanghai, China
1995

Federal Design Achievement Award
Presidential Design Awards
Independence Square
Washington, DC
1995

Building Design Excellence Award
GSA Design Awards
US Courthouse
Portland, Oregon
1994

ULI Award for Excellence
Large-scale office buildings
Washington Mutual Tower
Seattle, Washington
1994

National AIA Honors Award
Westendstrasse 1
Frankfurt am Main, Germany
1994

Design Award
New York State AIA
Westendstrasse 1
Frankfurt am Main, Germany
1994

Distinguished Architecture Award
New York Chapter AIA
Westendstrasse 1
Frankfurt am Main, Germany
1994

**Long Term Commitment to Design
Excellence and Application of Technology
Award**
Construction Specifications Institute
Kohn Pedersen Fox Associates PC
New York, New York
1994

Recognition Award
Buildings Magazine's 1994 Modernization
660 Madison/Barneys New York
New York, New York
1994

Dallas Urban Design Award
Urban Design
Federal Reserve Bank of Dallas
Dallas, Texas
1993

Prix d'excellence
Design Excellence
1250 Boulevard René Lévesque
Montreal, Canada
1993

Distinguished Architecture Award
New York Chapter AIA
1250 Boulevard René Lévesque
Montreal, Canada
1993

Distinguished Architecture Award
Houston Chapter AIA
Federal Reserve Bank of Dallas
Dallas, Texas
1993

Prix Orange
Save Montreal
1250 Boulevard René Lévesque
Montreal, Canada
1992

Distinguished Architecture Category Citation
New York Chapter AIA
311 South Wacker Drive
Chicago, Illinois
1991

Design Citation
38th Annual *Progressive Architecture* Awards
The World Bank
Washington, DC
1991

Excellence of Design Award
New York State AIA
1325 Avenue of the Americas
New York, New York
1990

Architectural Firm Award
AIA
Kohn Pedersen Fox Associates PC
1990

Gold Medal of Honor Award
New York Chapter AIA
Kohn Pedersen Fox Associates PC
1989

Design Award Citation
New York Chapter AIA
Carwill House
Stratton, Vermont
1989

Design Award
36th Annual *Progressive Architecture* Awards
Rockefeller Plaza West
New York, New York
1989

Design Award
New York State AIA
Heron Tower
New York, New York
1988

Design Award
35th Annual *Progressive Architecture* Awards
Mainzer Landstrasse 58
Frankfurt am Main, Germany
1988

Design Award
34th Annual *Progressive Architecture* Awards
Station Center
White Plains, New York
1987

National AIA Honors Award
Procter & Gamble General Offices
Complex
Cincinnati, Ohio
1987

Design Award of Merit
New York State AIA
Hyatt Regency
Greenwich, Connecticut
1987

Friends of Downtown Award
Best New Building Design
333 Wacker Drive
Chicago, Illinois
1986

What Might Be Award
New York City Chapter AIA
Station Center
White Plains, New York
1986

Merit Award
New York State Chapter AIA
General Re Corporate Headquarters
Stamford, Connecticut
1986

Award for Design Excellence
New York State Chapter AIA
One Logan Square
Philadelphia, Pennsylvania
1985

Distinguished Architecture Award
New York Chapter AIA
ABC-TV Studios 23/24
New York, New York
1985

National AIA Honors Award
333 Wacker Drive
Chicago, Illinois
1984

Distinguished Architecture Award
New York Chapter AIA
Hercules Incorporated Headquarters
Wilmington, Delaware
1984

Exhibitions

MIPIM ASIA 97
Singapore International Convention
and Exhibition Centre
Suntec City, Singapore
September 16–18, 1997

MIPIM 97
Le Palais des Festivals
Cannes, France
March 14–17, 1997

MIPIM 96
Le Palais des Festivals
Cannes, France
March 14–17, 1997

US Construction & Design Fair
US Trade Center
Tokyo & Nagoya, Japan
September 27, 1995

MIPIM 95
Le Palais des Festivals
Cannes, France
March 9–12, 1995

AIA "CAN STRUCTION"
Decoration & Design Building
New York, New York
November 10–17, 1994

The Art of the KPF Family
KPF Gallery
New York, New York
November 1–28, 1994

Career Day in Architecture
The Roosevelt Hotel on Madison Avenue
New York, New York
October 29, 1994

US Construction & Design Fair
US Foreign Commercial Service in
cooperation with American Chamber of
Commerce in Japan
Architecture, Engineering & Construction
Subcommittee
Fukuoka, Japan
September 9, 1994
Osaka, Japan
September 14, 1994
Tokyo, Japan
September 16, 1994

Building for Future
Six New Courthouses
26 Federal Plaza
New York, New York
August 18 – September 22, 1994

Barn Again!
National Building Museum
Washington, DC
March–September 1994

MIPIM 94
Le Palais des Festivals
Cannes, France
March 11–14, 1994

**Chicago Architecture and Design
1923–1993:
Reconfiguration of an American Metropolis**
Art Institute of Chicago
Chicago, Illinois
June 12 – August 29 1993

New Chicago Architecture
Chicago Athenaeum
Chicago, Illinois
January 29, 1991

Salon International de l'Architecture SIA 90
Grande Halle de la Villette
Paris, France
KPF featured
October 27 – November 4, 1990

Design USA
(Travelling USIA Exhibit)
USSR: Moscow, Leningrad, Donetsk,
Kishinev, Dushanbe, Alma-Ata, Novosibirsk,
Khabarovsk, Vladivostok
KPF featured
September 1989 – May 1991

Centennial Exhibit
University of Pennsylvania
Philadelphia, Pennsylvania
September 14 – November 4, 1990

New York Architecture 1970–1990
The Architecture Museum
Frankfurt, Germany
MOPU Gallery of the Ministerio de Obras
Publicas y Urbanismo
Madrid, Spain
Museo De Costumbres Populares
Seville, Spain
Taipei Fine Arts Museum
Taipei, Taiwan
KPF featured
1990

**Architecture for the City:
Kohn Pedersen Fox**
Minnesota Museum of Fine Art
St Paul, Minnesota
August 5 – September 23, 1990
KPF only

Celebrate Chicago Architecture
Union Station
Washington, DC
KPF featured
June 26 – July 20, 1990

The Panorama of New York City
Queens Museum
New York, New York
KPF featured
June 20, 1990

AIA Exhibit
George R. Brown Convention Center
Houston, Texas
KPF featured as the Architectural Firm of
the Year
May 18–21, 1990

Blueprints for Growth
AIA
Portland, Oregon
KPF only
May 1, 1990

Architecture in Boston 1975–1990
(50th Anniversary meeting of the Society of
Architectural Historians)
Bank of Boston
Boston, Massachusetts
KPF featured
March 27 – May 17, 1990

Building by Design: Architecture at IBM
National Building Museum
Washington, DC
KPF featured
March 21 – September 30, 1990

**On the Waterfront: Site Sensitive Building
by the Chicago River**
ArchiCenter Gallery
Chicago, Illinois
March 13 – May 19, 1990

Accent on Architecture
(Exhibit for Kohn Pedersen Fox to receive
the 1990 Architectural Firm Award)
National AIA
Washington, DC
February 22, 1990

New Chicago Skyscrapers
Chicago Athenaeum
Chicago, Illinois
October 30 – December 5, 1989

Tall Buildings Exhibition
Allendale Square
Perth, Australia
October 13–21, 1989

Museum of Architecture
Frankfurt, Germany
March 3, 1989

Collegiate School
New York, New York
September–November 1988

Desseins sur Montreal 2
International Biennial in Urban Design
Complexe Guy-Farreau
Montreal, Canada
September–October 1988

Excellence in Design
New York State AIA
New York, New York
September 1988

135 Years and Still Growing
St Paul Companies
St Paul, Minnesota
KPF only
August–November 1988

Experimental Skytowers
Rizzoli International Bookstore and Gallery
Watertower Place
Chicago, Illinois
August–September 1988

New Chicago Skyscraper Exhibit
Chicago Architectural Foundation
ArchiCenter Gallery
Chicago, Illinois
July 11 – September 7, 1988

10 on 10: The Critics Choice
The Urban Center
New York, New York
May–June, 1988

100 Years, 100 Architects
Gallery MA
Tokyo, Japan
Tojusu Center, KPF Room
Osaka, Japan
April 1988

A + U Exhibit
Tokyo, Japan
April 1988

**The Current Architecture of Kohn
Pedersen Fox**
Gallery of Design at the Merchandise Mart
Chicago, Illinois
KPF only
February 25 – March 18, 1988

**Window Display for "Kohn Pedersen Fox:
Buildings and Projects 1976–1987"**
Rizzoli International Bookstore
New York, New York
KPF only
February 2–16, 1988

**Window Display for "Kohn Pedersen Fox:
Buildings and Projects 1976–1987"**
Scribner and Sons Bookstore
New York, New York
KPF only
January 12–26, 1988

**Hyatt Regency Hotel
Special Recognition Award**
Concrete Industry Board of New York
26th Annual Awards Dinner
New York, New York
November 17, 1987

Prestressed PCI
New Orleans, Louisiana
October 1987

Procter & Gamble General Offices
Complex Honor Award Display
1987

Sketches • Ink Drawings • Renderings
Ballenford Architectural Books and Gallery
Toronto, Canada
KPF only
November 16, 1987 – December 31, 1987

New New York
Queens Museum
New York, New York
July 30 – September 12, 1987

Original Drawings & Models Exhibition
National Academy of Design/New York
Chapter AIA
New York, New York
May 14 – June 28, 1987

New York Academy of Design
New York, New York
May 1987

Portals: Points of Entry
Valencia Community College
Orlando, Florida
May–June 1987

GA International '87
GA Gallery
Tokyo, Japan
April 25 – May 31, 1987

Heritage Preservation Scholarship
New York City AIA
Architectural Heritage Ball
Urban Center
New York, New York
1986

Lieux de Travail
Centre Georges Pompidou
Paris, France
June 25 – October 13, 1986

**Critical Alternatives for Architecture in the
Next Decade**
MODERN REDUX
Grey Art Gallery and Study Center
New York University
New York, New York
March 3 – April 10, 1986

Award of Merit for Architectural Design
1986

The Architecture of Kohn Pedersen Fox
NCSU School of Design
KPF only
February 19 – March 10, 1986

National Academy of Design
New York, New York
February 1986

Municipal Art Society
New York, New York
January 1986

**Photo panels at New York City Chapter AIA
Members Headquarters Gallery**
New York, New York
January 22 – February 20, 1986

**1985 New York City Chapter AIA Unbuilt
Awards Program**
Exhibit at the National Academy of Design
New York, New York
January 22 – February 13, 1986

South Ferry Plans and Proposals
Urban Center
New York, New York
December 9, 1985 – January 4, 1986

Harvard University
Boston, Massachusetts
KPF only
November 26 – December 7, 1985

Lost and Won Competitions
AIA
San Francisco, California
1985

Award for Excellence in Design 1985
Rochester Plaza Hotel
Rochester, New York
October 19, 1985

Craft in Architecture
New York State Association of Architects/
AIA Annual Convention
New York, New York
October 1985

Architex '85
Barbican Exhibition Centre
London, England
June 26–28, 1985

The Works of Kohn Pedersen Fox
Royal Institute of British Architects
London, England
KPF only
June 10 – July 9, 1985

**1985 Distinguished Architecture
Awards Exhibit**
New York City Chapter AIA
Municipal Arts Society, Urban Center
New York, New York
May 15 – June 15, 1985

**Exhibition of Work by Newly Elected
Members and Recipients of Awards**
Arnold W. Brunner Memorial Prize in
Architecture
American Academy and Institute of Arts
and Letters
New York, New York
KPF only
May 15 – June 1985

Selected Works
Baltimore Museum of Art for the Baltimore
Chapter AIA
Baltimore, Maryland
KPF only
March 4 – April 29, 1985

**Buildings in Progress Since
Midtown Zoning**
Municipal Art Society, Urban Center
New York, New York
January–February 1985

Honor Award
AIA
1984

**New York City AIA Architectural Drawings
Award Exhibit**
New York, New York
1984

AIA Annual Members Exhibit
Philadelphia Chapter AIA
Philadelphia, Pennsylvania
1983

Calgary Exhibit
KPF only
1983

San Francisco, Bill Pedersen Exhibit
KPF only
1983

Project Credits

333 Wacker Drive, Chicago
Owner: Urban Investment &
Development Co.
Architect of Record: Perkins & Will, Chicago
Project Principal: A. Eugene Kohn
Design Principal: William Pedersen
Design Team Leader: Alexander Ward
Project Manager: Gary Stluka

Procter & Gamble General Offices Company Complex
Owner: Procter & Gamble
Project Principal: A. Eugene Kohn
Design Principal: William Pedersen
Management Principal: Robert Cioppa
Planning Principal: Patricia Conway
Design Team Leaders: Alexander Ward,
Craig B. Nealy
Project Managers: Timothy Hartley,
Lee Polisano
Coordination Leader: Benedict Curatolo

Goldman Sachs European Headquarters, Peterborough Court
Owner: LDT Partners
Architect of Record: EPR Architects Ltd,
London
Project Principals: A. Eugene Kohn,
Lee Polisano
Design Principal: William Pedersen
Design Team Leader: Craig B. Nealy
Project Manager: James E. Outen
Coordination Leader: Peter Tao
Team: Robin Andrade, Carol Buhrmann,
Joshua Chaiken, Karen Cook, Roger
Cooner, John Crellin, Susan Davis-
McCarter, Miriana Doneva, Angeline Ho,
Jane Murphy, Mark Nosky, Stephanie
Spoto, Margaret Walker

Westendstrasse 1/DG Bank Headquarters
Owner: Agima Aktiengesellschaft für
Immobilien-Anlage mbH
Architect of Record: Nägele Hofmann
Tiedemann + Partner, Frankfurt
Project Principals: A. Eugene Kohn,
Lee Polisano
Design Principal: William Pedersen
Design Team Leader: Paul King
Project Manager: Andreas Hausler
Team: William Davis, Robert Demel,
Armando Gutierrez, George Hauner, John
Koga, Nicole Mronz, Jane Murphy, Evelyn
Neumann, Wolfgang Neumüller, Beth
Niemi, James Papoutsis, Klaus Zahn,
Birgit Zwankhuizen

1250 Boulevard René-Lévesque/IBM Quebec Headquarters
Owner: Marathon Real Estate Ltd and
IBM Canada Ltd
Architect of Record: LaRose Petrucci
& Associés, Montreal
Project Principal: A. Eugene Kohn
Design Principal: William Pedersen
Design Team Leader: Richard Clarke
Project Manager: Sudhir Jambhekar
Coordination Leader: Glen DaCosta
Team: Carol Buhrmann, Miriana Doneva,
Bruce Eisenberg, John Koga, Carlos
Menendez, Stephanie Spoto

Rockefeller Plaza West
Owner: Rockefeller Center Development
Corporation
Design Principal: William Pedersen
Management Principal: Robert Cioppa
Design Team Leaders: Paul Gates, Paul Kevin
Kennon
Project Manager: Gregory Clement
Coordination Leader: George Hauner
Team: Kevin Batchelor, Alex Bergo, Alexis
Briski, Max Cardillo, Mark Chaney, Ben
Cherner, Enrico Cordice, Mark Costandi,
John Crellin, Marjann Dumoulein,
Dominic Dunn, Valerie Edozien, Robert
Furno, Robert Goodwin, Peter Gross,
Armando Gutierrez, Tomas Hernandez,
Eloise Marinos, Darcy Rathjen, Francisco
Rencoret, Erika Schmitt, John Stoltze,
Hisaya Sugiyama, Ed Tachibana,
Andrew Vines

Newport Harbor Art Museum
Owner: Newport Harbor Art Museum
Project Principal: A. Eugene Kohn
Design Principal: William Pedersen
Management Principal: Robert Cioppa
Design Team Leaders: Paul Katz, Sulan
Kolatan, Josh Chaiken
Project Manager: Christopher Keeny
Team: Kevin Batchelor, Mary Sue Gaffney,
Sulan Kolatan, Malvina Lampietti,
Esmatollah Seraj, Thomas Vandenbout
Associate Architect: Gruen Associates, Los
Angeles

Carwill House II
Owner: William and Carolyn Stutt
Design Principal: William Pedersen
Design Team Leader: Joshua Chaiken
Project Manager: Alex Bergo
Team: Tzadik Eliakim, John Fernandez,
Armando Gutierrez, Cecelia Kramer,
Anthony Mosellie, Kia Pedersen, Denise
Vanderlind, Susan Seastone

Federal Reserve Bank of Dallas
Owner: Federal Reserve Bank of Dallas
Architect of Record: Sikes Jennings Kelly
& Brewer, Houston, Texas
Project Principal: A. Eugene Kohn
Design Principal: William Pedersen
Design Team Leader: Richard Clarke
Coordination Leader: Glen DaCosta
Team: Tat Chan, Marjann Dumoulein,
Alex Gotz, Joel Karr, Ming Leung,
Tzen-Ying Ling, Nicole Mronz,
Ryoichi Nakamora, Susan Seastone,
John Sheffield, Thomas Vandenbout,
Robert Whitlock

World Bank Headquarters
Owner: The International Bank for
Reconstruction & Development
(The World Bank)
Project Principals: A. Eugene Kohn,
Sheldon Fox
Design Principal: William Pedersen
Design Team Leader: Craig B. Nealy
Project Managers: Thomas Holzmann,
William H. Cunningham
Coordination Leader: Joseph P. Ruocco
Team: Robin Andrade, Isabelle Autones,
Dayo Babalola, Pavel Balla, Vladimir Balla,
Joseph Barnes, Mark Barnhouse, Gabrielle
Blackman, Nathan Clark Corser, Suzanne
Cregan, Cynthia Crier, Glen DaCosta, Eric
Daum, Anthony DiGrazia, Dominic Dunn,
Valerie Edozien, Mark Fiedler, Robin
Goldberg, Armando Gutierrez, Fia
Hekmat, Angeline Ho, Koichiro Ishiguro,
Sulan Kolatan, Judy Lee, Ming Leung,
Jenny Ling, Michael Martin, Kristen
Minor, Nicole Mronz, Beth Niemi, Hun
Oh, James Papoutsis, Paul Regan, Duncan
Reid, James Seger, Esmatollah Seraj,
Audrey Shen, Frank Shenton, Emil
Stojakovitch, John Stoltze, Hisaya
Sugiyama David Thompson,
Thomas Vandenbout
Competition Team Contributor:
Peter Schubert
Associate Architect: Kress Cox Associates,
Washington, DC

First Hawaiian Center
Owner: First Hawaiian Bank
Developer: The Myers Corporation
Design Principals: William Pedersen,
Peter Schubert
Project Manager: Charles Alexander
Coordination Leaders: Deborah Booher,
Bun-Wah Nip, Kristin Minor
Team: Barbara Bures, Celia Chiang,

Carey Chu, Irvin Glassman, Robert Goodwin, Armando Gutierrez, Tomas Hernandez, Barbara Lewandowska, Malvina Lampietti, Elaine Newman, Molly McGowan, Marcie Moss, Ichiro Oda, Dex Ott, Glenn Rescalvo, Erica Schmitt, Audrey Shen, Joseph Spada

US Courthouse, Portland
Owner: General Services Administration
Architect of Record: BOORA Architects, Portland, Oregon
Design Principal: William Pedersen
Management Principal: Robert Cioppa
Design Team Leader: Jerri Smith with Gabrielle Blackman and Doug Hocking
Project Manager: Sudhir Jambhekar
Team: Juan Alayo, Isabelle Autones, Christine Awad, Vladimir Balla, Nathan Clark Corser, Vivian Kuan, Trent Tesch

Aid Association for Lutherans Headquarters Expansion
Owner: Aid Association for Lutherans
Design Principal: William Pedersen
Management Principal: Robert Cioppa
Design Team Leader: Beth Niemi
Project Manager: Paul Pichardo
Coordination Leader: Nathan Clark Corser
Team: Vladimir Balla, Christine Bruckner, Verica Cameron, Carey Chu, Marianne Kwok, Mimi Love

Greater Buffalo International Airport
Owner: Niagara Frontier Transportation Authority
Joint Venture: Cannon Design Inc., William Nicholas Bodouva + Associates, and Kohn Pedersen Fox Associates
Project Principal: A. Eugene Kohn
Design Principal: William Pedersen
Design Team Leaders: Duncan Reid, Richard Clarke
Project Manager: Anthony Mosellie
Coordination Leaders: Lucinda Dip, Peter Gross, Bun-Wah Nip
Team: Philip Brown, Carey Chu, Christopher Ernst, Kar-Hwa Ho, Brian Kaufman, I-Ann Lin, Elaine Newman, William Vinyard

Dacom Headquarters Building
Owner: Dacom Corporation
Architect of Record: Chang-Jo Corporation, Seoul, Korea
Design Principal: William Pedersen
Design Team Leader: John Koga
Coordination Leader: Glen DaCosta
Team: Verica Cameron, Angela Davis,

Kurt Dannwolf, Nazila Shabestari Duran, Garrett Finney, Tomas Hernandez, Jen-Suh Hou, Katherine Kennedy, Eun Kyong Kim, Chulhong Min, Roy Pachecano

Shanghai World Financial Center
Owner: Forest Overseas Co. Ltd
Architect and Engineer of Record: Shimizu Corporation
Project Principal: A. Eugene Kohn
Design Principal: William Pedersen
Management Principal: Paul Katz
Design Team Leader: Joshua Chaiken
Project Coordinator: Hisaya Sugiyama
Coordination Leader: Mabel Tse
Team: Gregory Waugh, David Weinberg, Hannelore Barnes, Christine Bruckner, Larry Burkes, Verica Cameron, Cathleen Chua, Mark Gausepohl, Rena Gyftopoulos, Tomas Hernandez, Doug Hocking, Jen-Suh Hou, Phanuwit Kanthatham, Vivian Kuan, Barbara Lewandowska, John Lucas, Methanee Maassirarat, William McNamara, Elaine Newman, Yayoi Ogo, Harutaka Oribe, Cordula Roser, Susana Su, Trent Tesch, Robert Thome, Nelson Tom, Suzan Wines, Shinichiro Yorita, Jason Zerafa
Project Architect and Engineer: Mori Building Architects & Engineers Ltd
Collaborative Architect: East China Architectural Design and Research Institute

SBS Competition
Owner: Seoul Broadcasting System
Design Principal: William Pedersen
Design Team Leader: Duncan Reid
Project Manager: Paul Pichardo
Team: Philip Brown, Nazila Shabestari Duran, Sae-Young Lee, Chulhong Min, Christopher Stoddard, Thomas Turturro
Associate Architect: Chang-Jo Corporation, Seoul, Korea

IBM World Headquarters
Owner: IBM
Project Principal: Gregory Clement
Design Principal: William Pedersen
Design Team Leaders: Jerri Smith, Douglas Hocking
Project Manager: Christopher Keeny
Coordination Leaders: Gregory Waugh, Simona Budeiri
Team: Christine Awad, Vladimir Balla, Darlington Brown, Christine Bruckner, Elina Cardet, Winston Anthony Edwards, Armando Gutierrez, Rena Gyftopoulos,

Markus Hahn, Charles Ippolito, David Kaplan, Ming Leung, John Locke, Harutaka Oribe, Yin Teh, Trent Tesch, Suzan Wines
Interiors Architect: Swanke Hayden Connell Ltd

Baruch College New Academic Complex
Owner: Baruch College, Dormitory Authority, State of New York, City University of New York
Design Principal: William Pedersen
Executive Project Managers: Jill Lerner, Anthony Mosellie
Design Team Leader: Gabrielle Blackman
Interior Project Designer: Mavis Wiggins
Interior Project Manager: Robert Hartwig
Coordination Leader: Lloyd Sigal
Interiors Coordination Leader: Marta Enebuske
Team: Gregory Clement, Paul Baird, Gary Brown, Christine Bruckner, Angela Davis, Christopher Ernst, Terri Figliuzzi, Tomas Hernandez, Jen-Suh Hou, Johannes Knoops, I-Ann Lin, Michael Marcolini, Methanee Massirarat, Yan Meng, Lynne Miyamoto, David Ottavio, Duncan Reid, Marie Richter, Cordula Roser, Jorge Septien, Christopher Stoddard, Gerald Sullivan, Yutaka Takiura, Paul Tarantino, Juliet Whelan, Thomas Yo, Julie Young
Associate Architect: Castro-Blanco Piscioneri

New Law School Building, University of Washington
Owner: University of Washington
Architect of Record: Mahlum & Nordfors McKinley Gordon, Seattle, Washington
Design Principal: William Pedersen
Project Principal: Gregory Clement
Design Team Leader: Jerri Smith
Project Manager: Nathan Clark Corser
Team: Susana Su, Trent Tesch

Daewoo Marina City 21/Suyoung Bay Landmark Tower Competition
Owner: Daewoo Corporation
Architect of Record: Namsan Architects & Engineers, Seoul, Korea
Project Principal: Robert Cioppa
Design Principal: William Pedersen
Design Team Leaders: Robert Whitlock, Tómas Alvarez
Project Manager: Chulhong Min
Team: Joshua Chaiken, Luke Fox, Eric Howeler, Marianne Kwok, John Lucas, Yujiro Yorita, Jason Zerafa

Rodin Pavilion at Samsung Headquarters Area Renovation

Owner: Samsung
Architect of Record: Samoo Architects & Engineers, Seoul, Korea
Project Principal: Gregory Clement
Design Principals: Paul Kevin Kennon, William Pedersen
Design Team Leaders: Marianne Kwok, Luke Fox
Project Managers: Andreas Hausler, John Locke
Coordination Leader: Francis Freire
Team: Vladimir Balla, Christopher Ernst, Andrew Kawahara, Michael Marcolini, Chulhong Min, Cordula Roser, Aida Saleh, Trent Tesch

Samyang Mixed-Use Building

Owner: Samyang Foods Company
Architect of Record: Chang-Jo Architects Inc., Seoul, Korea
Design Principals: William Pedersen, Peter Schubert
Design Team Leader: Roger Klein
Project Managers: Laurie Butler, Chulhong Min
Coordination Leader: Glen DaCosta
Team: Isabelle Algor, Luke Fox, Francis Freire, Jen-Suh Hou, Eun Kyong Kim, David Lukes, Lisa Ross, Scott Teman

General Re Corporate Headquarters

Owner: General Re Corporation
Project Principal: Sheldon Fox
Design Principal: William C. Louie
Design Team Leader: Chao-Ming Wu
Project Manager: Creighton Jones
Coordination Leader: Deborah Booher

Mellon Bank Center

Owner: Richard I. Rubin & Company Inc. and Equitable Life Assurance Society of the United States
Project Principal: A. Eugene Kohn
Design Principal: William C. Louie
Design Team Leader: Peter Schubert
Project Managers: Jan Gleysteen, Myron Sigal
Coordination Leader: Deborah Booher
Team: Christine Awad, Anthony Barnaba, Annabel Delgado, Miriana Doneva, Michael Fontaine, James Jorganson, Carlos Menendez, Shi Foo Peng, Audrey Shen, Jerri Smith, James von Klemperer, Chao-Ming Wu, Vladislav Zacek

Chifley Tower

Owner: Kumagai (NSW) Pty Ltd (Original owner: Bond Corporation)
Project Principal: A. Eugene Kohn
Design Principal: William C. Louie
Design Team Leaders: Christopher Keeny, Yolanda Cole
Project Manager: Robert Busler
Team: Vladimir Balla, Mark Barnhouse, Roger Cooner, John Duvall, Reade Elliott, Michael Fontaine, Joseph Furio, Robert Goodwin, Genevieve Gormley, William LaPatra, Eugenia Merkulova, Beth Niemi, Andrew Pollack, August Schaefer, Hilde Schneider, Scott Specht, Emil Stojakovic, Lillian Tay, Vivian Volz, Gregory Waugh
Associate Architect: Travis Partners Pty Ltd, Sydney

Foley Square Courthouse

Owner: BPT Properties Foley Square, LP
Project Principals: A. Eugene Kohn, Robert Cioppa
Design Principal: William C. Louie
Design Team Leader: James von Klemperer
Project Manager: Christopher Keeny
Coordination Leader: Gregory Waugh
Team: Izai Amorim, Vladimir Balla, Richard Berdan, Alexis Briski, Lori Clark, Duncan Brown, Karen Dauler, Deborah Delnevo, Robert Dick, Lucinda Dip, Mark Fiedler, Terri Figliuzzi, Robert Goodwin, Peter Gross, Armando Gutierrez, James Hawley, Tomas Hernandez, Tatiana Kasnar, Rob Lane, John Lucas, Anthony Mosellie, Russell Patterson, Margaret Rice, Gerard Robertson, Michael Rose, Erika Schmitt, Gabriella Schumacher, Susan Seastone, Audrey Shen, Stephanie Spoto, George Sucato, Scott Teman, David Thompson, Jeffrey Wagenbach, Robert Whitlock, Mavis Wiggins, Jarvis Wong
Associate Architect: Simmons Architects

Ceres Master Plan for New Town

Owner: San Ju Corporation
Design Principal: William C. Louie
Design Team Leader: James von Klemperer
Project Manager: John Lucas
Team: Peter Gross, Dawn Parker Heifetz, Vivian Kuan, Qingyun Ma, Robert Whitlock

Bank Niaga Headquarters

Owner: Bank Niaga
Architect of Record: P.T. Wiratman & Associates, Jakarta, Indonesia
Project Principal: Robert Cioppa

Design Principal: William C. Louie
Design Team Leader: James von Klemperer
Coordination Leader: Roger Cooner
Team: Joseph Barnes, Cynthia Crier, Marjann Dumoulein, Valerie Edozien, Tzadik Eliakim, Howe Keen Foong, Joseph Furio, Joel Karr, Lucien Keldany, Sharon Lahr, Scott Specht, Scott Teman, Robert Whitlock

Yuksamdong

Owner: Dongbu Corporation
Architects of Record: Baum Architects Engineers Consultants and Hahn International, Architects
Design Principals: William C. Louie, James von Klemperer
Management Principal: Gregory Clement
Project Manager: Thomas Holzmann
Coordination Leader: Peter Gross
Team: Christine Bruckner, Verica Cameron, Rebecca Carpenter, Celia Chiang, Lucinda Dip, Dawn Parker Heifetz, Vivian Kuan, Qingyun Ma, Chulhong Min

Seocho Fashion Center

Owner: Samsung
Architect of Record: Samoo Architects & Engineers, Seoul, Korea
Design Principal: William C. Louie
Design Team Leader: Robert Goodwin
Executive Project Manager: Jill Lerner
Project Manager: Peter Gross
Coordination Leader: Christine Bruckner
Team: Carey Chu, Jason DePierre, Jen-Suh Hou, Dohee Lee, Richard Lee, Sae-Young Lee, Chulhong Min, Joshua Penn Ruderman, Scott Schiamberg, Raquel Sendra, Nelson Tom, Gary Turton, Thomas Turturro, Marguerite Wiltshire

Taichung Tower: Schemes I and II

Owner: Tzung Tang Development Group Co. Ltd
Architect of Record: Chang & Jan, Architects & Planners
Project Principal: A. Eugene Kohn
Design Principal: William C. Louie

Scheme I

Design Team Leader: Robert Goodwin
Project Manager: Robert Busler, Anthony Mosellie
Coordination Leader: Simona Budeiri, Lloyd Sigal
Team: Dawn Burcaw, Mark Chaney, Dawn Parker Heifetz, Vivian Kuan, Jenny Ling, Walter Lorenzut, Dex Ott, Scott Teman, David Thompson, Irene Yu

Scheme II
Design Team Leader: Robert Goodwin
Project Manager: Peter Gross
Coordination Leader: Bun-Wah Nip
Team: Gustavo Arango, Monika Brugger,
Carol Chang, Pei Yu Chen, Sophia Chen,
Nazila Schabestari Duran, Christopher
Ernst, Patrick Hwang, Carrie Johnson,
Michael Levy, Aida Saleh, Alberto
Sellenberger, Ehrmei Yuan

Menara Mulpha Headquarters
Owner: Mulpha International Sdn. Bhd.
Architect of Record: Akipraktis, Kuala
Lumpur
Design Principal: William C. Louie
Design Team Leader: Robert Whitlock
Project Manager: David Weinberg
Team: Monika Brugger, Helmut Dippold,
Eric Rich, Hugh Trumbull

**Hongkong Electric Company Head
Office Redevelopment**
Owner: Hongkong Electric Company
Architect of Record: Hsin Yieh Architects &
Associates Ltd
Design Principal: William C. Louie
Management Principal: Paul Katz
Design Team Leader: Hugh Trumbull
Project Manager: Peter Gross
Team: Hannelore Barnes, Monika Brugger,
J. Gregorio Brugnoli, Nazila Shabistari
Duran, Christopher Ernst, Widia Ranti
Hendratmo, Terence Koh, Richard Lee,
Methanee Massirarat, Cordula Roser,
Yutaka Takiura, Thomas Turturro

Bloomingdale's
Owner: Federated Department Stores,
Bloomingdale's
Project Principal: A. Eugene Kohn
Design Principal: Paul Kevin Kennon
Design Team Leaders: Charles Ippolito,
Marianne Kwok, Nicola Walter, Jason
Zerafa
Project Managers: Laurie Butler, David
Weinberg (Sherman Oaks & Century
City), Nathan Clark Corser, David Kaplan,
Andreas Hausler (Aventura)
Coordination Leaders: Angeline Ho, Bun-
Wah Nip
Team: J. Gregorio Brugnoli, Elina Cardet,
Cathleen Chua, Kurt Dannwolf, Angelo
Directo, Luke Fox, Rena Gyftopoulos,
Charles Ippolito, Lori Kellner, Ming
Leung, Michael Levy, Michael Marcolini,
Chulhong Min, Yayoi Ogo, Dex Ott, Widia
Ranti, Cordula Roser, Lisa Ross, Aida

Saleh, Joseph Spada, Christopher
Stoddard, Thomas Turturro
Associate Architects: Architects Pacifica
(Century City), Associated Architects &
Planners (Sherman Oaks)

G.T. International Tower
Owner: Philippine Securities Corporation
Executive Project Director: Paul Katz
Design Team Leader: Craig B. Nealy
Project Manager: Thomas Holzmann
Coordination Leader: Russell Patterson
Team: Paul Baird, Armando Gutierrez,
Eric Howeler, Michael Levy
Associate Architect: G F & Partners

JR Central Towers
Owner: Central Japan Railway Co.
Project Principal: A. Eugene Kohn
Management Principal: Paul Katz
Design Team Leader: John Koga
Project Manager: Michael Greene
Coordination Leader: Roger Cooner
Team: Christine Awad, Dawn Burcaw,
Carey Chu, Jerry Conduff, Milton Curry,
Thomas Demetrion, John Lucas, Lucinda
Dip, Mary Sue Gaffney, Yukio Hasegawa,
Tomas Hernandez, Douglas Hocking,
Akiko Jacobson, Paul Kevin Kennon,
Kristen Minor, James Moustafellos, Glenn
Rescalvo, Erika Schmitt, Lloyd Sigal, Emil
Stojakovic, Hisaya Sugiyama, Edward
Tachibana, Shinichiro Yorita
Project Architect and Engineer: Taisei
Corporation, Tokyo, Japan
Associate Architect: Seizo Sakata, Sakakura
Associates, Tokyo, Japan

The Landmark, Hong Kong
Owner: The Hongkong Land Property
Company Ltd
Project Principal: A. Eugene Kohn
Design Team Leader: John Koga
Executive Project Manager: Paul Katz
Project Manager: William Schweber
Coordination Leader: Dawn Parker Heifetz
Team: Danny Chong, Carey Chu, Peter
Gross, Jen-Suh Hou, Shinichi Shimomura,
Thomas Turturro
Associate Architect: P + T Architects
and Engineers

Niaga Tower II
Owner: P.T. Grahaniaga Tatautama, Niaga
Tower Partnership
Architect of Record: Atelier 6, Jakarta,
Indonesia
Project Principal: William C. Louie

Design Principal: James von Klemperer
Project Manager: Michael Greene
Coordination Leaders: Isabelle Autones,
Tatiana Kasnar
Team: Tómas Alvarez, Andrew
Bernheimer, Celia Chiang, Jisop Han,
Dohee Lee, Widia Hendratmo Ranti,
Susana Su, Gary Turton

Nanjing Xi Lu
Owner: Hang Lung Development Co. Ltd
Architect of Record: Mr Frank C. Y. Feng
Architects & Associates (HK) Ltd
Project Principal: A. Eugene Kohn
Design: William C. Louie and James
von Klemperer
Executive Project Manager: Paul Katz
Project Manager: William Schweber
Coordination Leader: Dominic Dunn
Team: Donna Barry, Andrew Bernheimer,
Carol Chang, Joy Chen, Larry Cohen,
Angelo Directo, Nazila Shabestari Duran,
Steven Frankel, Armando Gutierrez, Rena
Gyftopoulos, Daniel Heuberger, Francisca
Insulza, John Lucas, Qingyun Ma, Tracy
Malfetano, Beth Niemi, Roy Pachecano,
Marie Richter, Joseph Spada, Kees Van
Der Sande, William Vinyard, Nicola Walter

KPFI, LONDON

27 Old Bond Street
Team: Barry Docker, Kevin Flanagan,
Grant Garner, Tracy Green, Gary Handel,
Andreas Hausler, Mark Johnston, Cindy
Marshall, Chris McDonald, Lee Polisano,
Howard Rosenberg, Pablo Seggiaro,
Peter Tao, Scott Wilson
Project Manager: Kajima UK
Structural Engineer: Waterman Partnership
Construction Consultant: Norman Lambert

The Cyprus House of Representatives
Team: Vanessa Bartulovic, Scott Berry,
Nikki Blustin, Pat Bryan, Nicola Devine,
Mark Gausepohl, Willemina Hagenauw,
Lars Hesselgren, Karen Hilton, Herman
Hotze, Katherine Kennedy, Steve King,
James Langford, David Leventhal, Neil
Merryweather, Ian Milne, Luc Monsigny,
John Morgan, Lucy O'Brien, Ross Page,
Kia Pedersen, Fred Pilbrow, Lee Polisano,
Peter Provost, Marcus Springer, Sarah
Susman, Nick Swannell, Teal Usher,
Dean Weeden
Associate Architect: D. Kythreotis
and Associates
Structural Engineer: KAL Engineering

Thames Court
Team: Simon Appleby, Vanessa Bartulovic, Nikki Blustin, Pat Bryan, Mary Anne Bull, John Bushell, J. William Davis, Nicola Devine, Bryan Duncan, Keb Garavito, John Gibson, Carl Gulland, Karen Hilton, Mark Kelly, Katherine Kennedy, Ursula Klein, William Lo, David Lukes, Gareth McLachan, Selina Mason, Neil Merryweather, Luc Monsigny, Colin Muir, Ross Page, Gareth Paterson, Lee Polisano, Tony Pryor, John Silva de Sousa, Marcus Springer, Nick Swannell, Peter Tao, Ian Walker, Andrew Waugh, Dean Weeden
Structural Consultant: Waterman Partnership
Cost Consultant: GK Associates
Services Engineers: Flack + Kurtz
Construction Manager: Mace Ltd

Kingdom Trade Center
Team: Sandra Coppin, Lars Hesselgren, Jane Kim, Steve King, James Langford, David Leventhal, Neil Merryweather, Gareth Paterson, Fred Pilbrow, Lee Polisano, Gareth Wilkins
Structure: Buro Happold

Centre International Rogier
Team: Yasmin Al-Ani, Niamh Billings, Pat Bryan, J. William Davis, Nicola Devine, Melissa Doughty, Kevin Flanagan, John Gambrill, Christina Garcia, Matthias Hagi, Lars Hesselgren, Steve King, Wolfgang Lechner, David Leventhal, Neil Merryweather, Lucy O'Brien, Ross Page, Fred Pilbrow, Lee Polisano, Eliseo Rabbi, Marcus Springer, Peter Tao, Richard Thomas, Gozi Wamuo
Associate Architect: Samyn & Partners
Structural Engineer: Ove Arup & Partners

Bismarckstrasse 101
Team: Yasmin Al-Ani, Ron Bakker, Karen Cook, Courtney Coyne, Lars Hesselgren, Sorina Kopp, David Leventhal, Lee Polisano, Eliseo Rabbi
Consultant Architect: Patzschke Klotz + Partners
Technical Project Manager: Ingenieursgesellschaft mbH Projektsteuerung + Bauberatung
Structural Engineer: Göppner + Soulas

Provinciehuis
Team: Hanny Aichman, Ron Bakker, Vanessa Bartulovic, Niamh Billings, Brenda Bowman, Craig Burns, Florence Coleman, Lynda Dossey, Kevin Flanagan, Lindsay Gwilliam, Willemina Hagenauw,

Claudia Hasselbach, Herman Hotze, Craig Kiner, Ursula Klein, David Leventhal, Robert Mathewson, Gareth Mclachlen, Neil Merryweather, Kevin O'Leary, Ross Page, Kia Pedersen, Lee Polisano, Howard Rosenberg, Katherine Soulas, Sarah Susman, Bernard Tulkens, Andrew Waugh, Dean Weeden, Anna Williamson
Associate Architect: LIAG Architekten en bouwadviseurs

Opel Kreisel
Team: Yanko Apostolov, Eva Brümmendorf, Karen Cook, Sandra Coppin, Gunter Dörr, Cristina Garcia, Andreas Hausler, Karen Hilton, Andrea Jung, Annette Kachel, Sacha Lewis, Neil Merryweather, Ross Page, Gareth Patterson, Lee Polisano, Eliseo Rabbi, Götz Schönfeld, Nick Swannell, Gozi Wamuo, Owen Williams
Associate Architect: Nägele Hofmann Tiedemann + Partner
Project Manager: WPV Baubetreuung GmbH

Forum Frankfurt
Team: Simon Appleby, Craig Burns, J. William Davis, Katherine Dean, Gunter Dörr, Astrid Fuhrmeister, Suzzanne Geiger, Andreas Hausler, Lars Hesselgren, Annette Kachel, Paul King, Ursula Klein, Cecilia Kramer, David Long, Cindy Marhall, Wolfgang Neumüller, William Pedersen, Lee A. Polisano, Michael Regan, Francisco Rencoret, Gerhard Rinkens, Marcus Springer, Brigit Zwankhuizen

Wave Tower
Team: Ron Bakker, Kieran Breen, Mary Anne Bull, Craig Burns, Kevin Flanagan, Zoe Gizara, Edgar Gonzalez, Willemina Hagenauw, Claudia Hasselbach, Katherine Kennedy, David Leventhal, Melody Mason, Robert Mathewson, Neil Merryweather, Kevin O'Leary, Gerhard Rinkens, Peter Tao, Richard Thomas, Bernard Tulkens
Associate Architect: Leigh & Orange (Thailand) Ltd
Structural, Mechanical and Electrical Engineer: Meinhardt (Thailand) Ltd

Wave-Sathorn Financial Tower
Team: Ron Bakker, Kieran Breen, Eunsook Choi, Melissa Doughty, Scott Falvey, Kevin Flanagan, Jon Gibson, Edgar Gonzalez, Ryan Harper, Claudia Hasselbach, Herman Hotze, David Leventhal, Leif Lomo, Melody Mason, Jennifer Mehler, Neil Merryweather, Ross Page, Jorg

Schiefelbein, George Soo, Dean Weeden, Gareth Wilkins
Associate Architect: Architects 49 Ltd
Structural Engineer: ACTEC

Wave House
Team: Simon Appleby, Kieran Breen, Eunsook Choi, Simon Close, Kevin Flanagan, Jeroen Gerats, Claudia Hasselbach, James Langford, David Leventhal, Neil Merryweather, Soo-In Oh, Ross Page, Götz Schönfeld, George Soo, Dean Weedon
Associate Architect: Architects 49 Ltd
Structural Engineer: ACTEC

KBB
Team: Yanko Apostolov, Eva Brummendorf, Eunsook Choi, Karen Cook, Astrid Fuhrmeister, Edgar Gonzalez, Peter Habegger, Andreas Hausler, Karen Hilton, Andrea Jung, Annette Kachel, Katherine Kennedy, David Long, Neil Merryweather, Graham Newell, Soo-in Oh, Robert Peebles, Ross Page, Gareth Paterson, Lee Polisano, Kristi Roger, Penn Ruderman, Götz Schönfeld, Nick Swanell, Stefan Ulrich, Dean Weeden
Project Manager: Arthur Andersen & Co GmbH
Mechanical Consultant: HL-Technik AG
Structural Consultant: Göppner + Soulas

Daelim International Headquarters
Team: Kieran Breen, Eunsook Choi, Bryan Duncan, Emily Emrick, Kevin Flanagan, Claudia Hasselbach, David Leventhal, Leif Lomo, Neil Merryweather, Soo-In Oh, Jörg Schiefelbein, Andrew Waugh
Structural and Mechanical Engineer: Ove Arup & Partners

Coolsingel
Team: Ron Bakker, Brenda Bowman, Kevin Flanagan, Jeroen Gerats, Kristy Graham, Claudia Hasselbach, Jane Kim, David Leventhal, Neil Merryweather, Emma Nsugbe, Ross Page, Gareth Paterson, George Soo, Dean Weedenw
Associate Architect: INBO adviseurs bouw

Institute for American Studies
Team: Vanessa Bartulovic, Scott Berry, Willemina Hagenauw, Claudia Hasselbach, Lars Hesselgren, Ursula Klein, David Leventhal, Selina Mason, Neil Merryweather, Fred Pilbrow, Lee Polisano, Howard Rosenberg, Richard Thomas, Richard Wright
Consultant: Flack & Kurtz

Acknowledgements

I would like to thank Ilona Rider, whose untiring efforts over a long period of time, at times against great odds, have truly made this book possible and as special as it is. She has been ably assisted, first by Lucy Riederer and then by Mason White.

The work that is shown in this book reflects the tremendous talent and efforts of the Principals, Senior Associate Partners, Associate Partners and the entire professional staff in both in the New York and London offices. Marjorie Rodney has been invaluable and key to the coordination of the works of the London office.

Many of our projects have also benefited from the contributions of Associate Architects. No project, however, can be a success without the leadership and contribution of the owners and clients whose desire for outstanding architecture has been inspiring. Today's buildings are extremely complex and require the very best engineering and technical consulting, and we have been fortunate to have worked with the world's outstanding structural, mechanical, electrical and plumbing engineers, and all of the many consultants from kitchen to curtainwall, elevators, parking, lighting and landscaping, whose contributions have been vital to the final outcome of these projects. The book therefore reflects not only the combined efforts of all these people, but also the strong support of all of the secretaries, administrative staff, and our outstanding marketing group, all of whom have helped in achieving the high quality that this book demonstrates.

The names obviously are too numerous to mention, but my partners and I want to thank all those who worked on this book, as well as the photographers, model makers, and renderers whose names are listed under Project Cedits. They have captured the essence of the designs with the images contained in this book.

Last, but certainly not least, I would like to thank The Images Publishing Group, and especially Alessina Brooks, Paul Latham, Rod Gilbert and Antony Lord for their truly exceptional patience and perseverance.

A. Eugene Kohn FAIA, RIBA, JIA
President

Index

Bold page numbers refer to projects
included in Selected Works